Praise for Blythe Grossberg

"Grossberg interweaves memoir, psychology, and exposé in this juicy yet sympathetic account.... This nuanced chronicle humanizes an oft-caricatured world."

—*Publishers Weekly*

"With compassion and humor, Grossberg details the cutthroat ways the elite try to catapult their children to the top no matter the monetary (or emotional) cost. Despite the glittering exterior of this lifestyle, Grossberg explores an underbelly of insecurity, pain, and dysfunction."

—*Town & Country Magazine*

"A sobering close-up of parental wealth and power."

—*Kirkus Reviews*

"Grossberg writes...incisively and movingly."

—*East Hampton Star*

"Grossberg's fascinating book offers a rare glimpse into the school struggles of the wealthiest kids in New York, reading *The Great Gatsby* and living through it at the same time."

—**Jordan Ellenberg, author of *How Not to be Wrong* and *Shape***

"Blythe Grossberg's illuminating memoir, *I Left My Homework in the Hamptons*, offers a riveting and heartfelt look into her time tutoring the children of some of the wealthiest families in New York City. With clarity and compassion, Grossberg illustrates how, in so many instances, just beneath the surface of these families' gilded social media images are much more complex stories that too often involve dysfunction, loneliness and heartbreak. Like all of the best memoirs, Grossberg's compelling personal story is unique, but includes elements that will resonate with all readers. I highly recommend it!"

—**Jane Healey, bestselling author of *The Beantown Girls***

"A fascinating book about the world of elite schools and students—the competition and stressors of the rich, the downside of too much wealth and too little joy—all told through the stories of the young people who live in this world by an engaging, gifted, and empathic storyteller. Part memoir, part sociological study of the rich, part a treatise on education in America...but 100% compelling. Despite the singularity of the students, the questions this book poses are universal. How much is too much? Why do we require students to master things they are not yet capable of doing? How does the education of the rich exacerbate problems of class, race, and equality in ways that might make broader solutions more difficult? I couldn't put it down."

—Ellen Braaten, PhD, author of *Bright Kids Who Can't Keep Up*, Associate Professor, Harvard Medical School

I Left My Homework in the Hamptons

Teaching the Children of the One Percent

BLYTHE GROSSBERG

HANOVER
SQUARE
PRESS

**HANOVER
SQUARE
PRESS™**

Recycling programs
for this product may
not exist in your area.

ISBN-13: 978-1-335-47520-6

I Left My Homework in the Hamptons

First published in 2021. This edition published in 2023.

Hanover Square Press
22 Adelaide St. West, 41st Floor
Toronto, Ontario M5H 4E3, Canada
HanoverSqPress.com
BookClubbish.com

Printed in U.S.A.

For J.D. and T.D.

Also by Blythe Grossberg

Asperger's Rules! How to Make Sense of School and Friends

Asperger's and Adulthood: A Guide to Working, Loving, and Living with Asperger's Syndrome

Focused: ADHD & ADD Parenting Strategies for Children with Attention Deficit Disorder

Making ADD Work: On-the-Job Strategies for Coping with Attention Deficit Disorder

Autism and Your Teen: Tips and Strategies for the Journey to Adulthood

Test Success: Test-Taking and Study Strategies for All Students, Including Those with ADD and LD

Applying to College for Students with ADD or LD: A Guide to Keep You (and Your Parents) Sane, Satisfied, and Organized Through the Admission Process

Asperger's Teens: Understanding High School for Students on the Autism Spectrum

I Left My Homework in the Hamptons

TABLE OF CONTENTS

AUTHOR'S NOTE

A note about the characters in this book: The characters are based on the nearly twenty years I spent working with thousands of students in New York City. I have changed the names and identifying details and created composite characters to protect the identities and privacy of the people in the book. This book has elements of memoir, which reflect the author's present recollections of experiences in the past. Some events have been compressed, and some dialogue has been re-created. I tried to represent with accuracy the world I portray. Human memory is not perfect, but my intent was always to render the characters, particularly the children at the heart of the book, with fidelity and humanity.

1

The Doors of Fifth Avenue Open

When I meet my first tutee, fifteen-year-old Sophie, she sweeps down a grand, winding staircase covered with white carpet. Her Park Avenue duplex is appointed entirely in white, from the couches to the shag carpet to the miniature poodles yapping at her feet. The short skirt of her private-school uniform flaps as she scoops up one of her dogs, orders it to be quiet, and tweaks the bow on its tiny head. Before we ascend to work on writing, her housekeepers, two Filipino women, ask us if we would like anything to eat or drink.

In her room, a pink gingham bedspread matches the fabric on her desk chair. Everything else is white and spotless. The usual mess of a teenager's room is nowhere in sight. She has neatly stacked up her school books, but they are the only sign of clutter. Even her flat-screen TV is stored behind a

wood console, and the only objects disturbing the white-
ness and pinkness of her space is her collection of Limoges boxes, carefully arranged at right angles to each other.
There is a photo in a crystal picture frame of her with her
dad taken at a golf tournament in the Hamptons. It is only
when she opens the built-in cabinets over her desk that I
see the magazine cutouts that clutter most teenagers' rooms
alongside photos of her friends wearing too much makeup,
dressed to the nines in designer dresses and high heels.

After getting out her copy of *The Great Gatsby,* she begins
to speak about her assignment: to write an expository essay
about whether Gatsby achieved the American dream. Her
two white dogs start barking again until one of the Filipino
women comes to hush them and haul them downstairs.

"I'm going to say that Gatsby did *not* achieve the dream,"
she says, "because that's what my teacher thinks." She pauses
for a minute and licks her lips nervously. "Unless you think
I should write something else."

We go back and forth talking about the ideas, and I can
sense that she's nervous that I think there's no one right answer. Instead, I ask her to find support in the text for her
contention that Gatsby failed to achieve the dream. She leafs
through the pages mechanically, her nails painted with glittering polish that she has half picked off. She reads the following passage about Gatsby's riotous, lavish parties:

"'Every Friday five crates of oranges and lemons arrived
from a fruiterer in New York—every Monday these same
oranges and lemons left his back door in a pyramid of pulp-
less halves.'"

She is ready to skip ahead, until I ask her to slow down

and think about this image. "My parents' kitchen looks like that during a party, too," she says. "All those lemon rinds next to the bar. And my mom almost looks like a wrung-out lemon after a long night." She realizes that partygoers have trampled Gatsby's house, just as they regularly trash her parents' Hamptons house in the summer, and that the result is a sense of lethargy and letdown. The passage seems to make sense to her and to connect to her personal experience.

She uses the intercom on the wall next to her desk to buzz her maids to bring up some green tea, which appears in a matter of minutes in porcelain cups and saucers with thin lemon wedges teetering on the rims. We eventually hammer out an outline, and I think she has done a good job coming up with an arguable thesis and marshaling some evidence from the text. She musters a faint smile as I leave.

"Or *did* Gatsby achieve the dream?" she wonders aloud.

I leave elated. This has been a heady experience—the green tea, the white dogs, and getting paid to talk about Gatsby. I never dreamed that all my years of reading and being made fun of for loving poetry in public high school would actually result in something lucrative and fulfilling.

My route to Sophie's house was a circuitous one. While earning my doctoral degree in psychology, I had two major problems. The easier of the two was rejecting Freudianism in favor of behavioral approaches after I deemed Freud out of touch with modern realities. The harder one was being able to afford new shoes, instead of walking with holes in both of my flats, or an iced coffee for the homeless man who lived in the lobby of my building in Park Slope, Brooklyn. Or even buy one for myself, for that matter. It was also hard to afford subway fare, hence the walking, hence the holes in my shoes. I had essentially discovered that while my Harvard undergraduate education had made me very well-read, it did not automatically earn me subway fare. That was my fault, though, as I had bypassed lucrative financial jobs to study psychology, while my husband, also an Ivy grad, had become a magazine editor. We had a lot of books packed into our shabby apartment. Still, I believed that psychology would unravel the mysteries of the human mind, everything from altruism to irrationality, and just peeking into these mysteries was worth more to me than a six- or seven-figure income.

I thought a great deal while treading the streets of New York in my worn-down soles, and I was fortunate enough to strike upon the idea of writing a dissertation about ADHD that helped pave my way to working with students with learning differences and ADHD. When I got a job as a learning specialist, a teacher who helps students with such learning differences, in an elite Manhattan private school at an annual salary of $54,500, I felt secure for the first time in a long time, even with a newborn to care for at home. After years of earning a subsistence income, I decided I needed something steadier now that I had a young one of my own. I had lived in New York for ten years, and I so far had been able to scrape by without dipping into the gig economy. But when my friend who taught at an Upper East Side girls' school asked if I'd help a sweet, stressed-out sophomore with writing, I was ecstatic. This was the kind of work I'd do for free. The idea of getting paid for it—and on top of my salary—was nirvana, almost unthinkable.

Back in rural Massachusetts where I grew up, kids used to cheat off me for nothing.

To enter the calm, secure, sedate Park Avenue lobby of the building where this girl lived was to enter a world that promised the freedom of the rich, the transcendence of an art museum, and the satisfaction of calming a nervous fifteen-year-old. Little did I know that Freud, whom I'd so casually rejected in graduate school, was lurking, waiting for me in the hushed, lily-filled interior of those Park Avenue buildings, where neuroses of all sorts waited.

After Sophie earns her first A on a paper, rocketing up magically from her usual B+, I become a bit of a hot commodity in the duplexes and brownstones of Brooklyn and Manhattan. I am like the restaurant that is so trendy it isn't even in Zagat's yet. Later, after I've found some more students to tutor, mothers refer to me as *their secret,* and one is upset that her daughter's rival's mother has found out about me, too. "But we discovered you," she wails.

A mother named Lisa, a banker who sails in Nantucket, makes me cringe by saying, "I know my daughter will be all right in high school now that we have Blythe." With that one declaration, she has telegraphed to her daughter, *You, darling, simply don't rate without the help of a tutor with a doctoral degree.* She has also sent the message to her daughter that *In every situation, it's necessary to purchase the right kind of help, just as you would shop for just the right Dooney & Bourke bag.* This attitude is widespread along Fifth Avenue, where a student once told me, explaining away his failing chemistry grade, "Don't worry—we're changing the tutor." The sailor's daughter, Lily, is one of the sweetest, best-tempered children I've ever met. Endowed with a tender heart and an ill-timed tendency to choke on pre-calc tests and in high-stakes squash tournaments, she is at the mercy of the viciousness of her private-school girls' clique and the relentlessness of her squash schedule. Her mother wants her to be as elegant as Audrey Hepburn with a slicing squash swing, but Lily is actually better than that. She is clear-sighted in a way that many people in her world are not, and she becomes a kind of juvenile Virgil, my guide to the purgatory of stressed-out Park Avenue. When I tutor kids who are reading *The Divine Comedy*, I often think of Lily, guiding me to the concentric circles of hell. When we sit down to work, her account of the travails of her day comes seeping out, and she tells me about the parties she has attended, half-present and half wishing that she were at home in bed watching *The Office*.

I follow her stories with wonder, looking admiringly at the gold silk dress that lies crumpled in her closet, the relic of a weekend spent dashing about Manhattan in stilettos when my only excursion was to the shaved-ice vendor on our corner. I am usually home with my son when I'm not working, as the point of working for me is not only professional pride but also what affords me the ability to spend time with him and my husband. The idea of spending my leisure time traipsing around New York is foreign to me, lost as I always am in graduate-school studies or work. In a strange capitalist calculus, I work to be at home.

Lily tells me there are house parties when parents are away, as they often are. She has friends who don't even know where their parents are at night, and there are parents who call their kids at 10:00 p.m. to tell them they're in another city and won't be back that night. This makes Fifth Avenue the perfect place to have a party. Even if housekeepers are present, their jobs rely on keeping the kids happy and not telling the parents what is really going on when they're not home. Kids at Lily's school rent out clubs run by sleazy promoters, and they charge admission from their classmates. There is no one minding the store at these clubs. During one tutoring session, Lily tells me, "I went to a school party at a club, and kids were hanging out on the rooftop," which, in her vernacular, means kids were having sex on the rooftop. I had no way of verifying Lily's story, but it seemed possible. The kids on Fifth Avenue do things all kids do, just in more extreme ways.

Lily and her friends can pay the steep admission prices to these types of parties. They have a lot of money at their disposal. At the private schools where I've worked there are kids who show up with $100 bills at bake sales and who bring Gold Cards on field trips. This earned one of my students a lot of derision at a corner Brooklyn bodega where he tried to buy a bagel with his father's Amex Gold Card. The other customers seemed amused to the point of being irate, and I was glad when we got out of there in one piece. (As it turns out, the store did not accept Gold Cards for two-dollar bagel purchases.)

Lily's and Sophie's parents routinely provide their kids with a lot of pocket money or just hand them their credit cards. High school–aged kids who attend tony private schools are usually allowed to go out to lunch, which in

Manhattan and parts of Brooklyn isn't cheap. They don't often eat in their schools' dining halls, and they roam around the city getting bubble teas, sushi rolls, and fifteen-dollar burgers. It is standard for these private-school students to pay at least a hundred dollars for a week of lunches, and that doesn't include the seven-dollar coffee drinks they get during breaks and after school.

These kids are gourmands at a young age. Sophie explains that "I simply can't go to college where I can't get a good cappuccino." For this reason, she cannot attend college outside of New York City or Los Angeles. These kids know the difference between the salad greens. "Oh, endives!" shouts one fifth grader upon approaching the salad bar at a private school where I work. I'd never imagined little kids could enjoy endives and brie so heartily.

The money goes to other things, too, of course. Years ago, it was cigarettes and, more recently, it's flavored oils for vaping. These ill-smelling oils are vended at local vape shops, and they have mysterious elements that can make the kids really sick. When e-cigarettes first appeared, teens rationalized that they were healthier than drinking or smoking regular cigarettes, not realizing that vaping can have damaging effects on young lungs and brains and can still result in nicotine addiction. Trevor, another kid I tutor, steals bongs and vape pens from a store on Third Avenue because he says the owners sold him a defective vape pen that they refused to take back.

When I tell him that vaping poses dangers to kids that we don't even know about, he responds, "That's the T, Blythe! A friend of mine had a seizure after vaping nicotine." When

I ask him if this incident made kids at his school less likely to vape, he says, "No, whenever I enter the bathrooms at school, I just hear that noise of the JUUL. I don't even pay attention anymore. It's like running water."

The young of Fifth Avenue aren't alone in this. Kids all across America are vaping (the figure is thought to be 37 percent of all high-school seniors but might be much higher), but these kids also have money for other things, such as gambling. Trevor's school friends who are seniors and above age eighteen started going to Off-Track Betting before its closure, dingy storefronts where people could legally bet on horse racing, and two of them are in hock to a bookie for debts related to online gambling. No matter, of course. They fret for a bit and then sell an $800 pair of shoes for $400 to pay off the menacing bookies. Online gambling is an increasing nightmare for kids, and the International Centre for Youth Gambling Problems and High-Risk Behaviours at McGill University estimates that about 4 percent of children have a gambling problem. Gaming online has made them addicted to taking risks in the virtual world, and rich kids have disposable cash that enables them to get into deeper debt.

They find other ways to burn through money online. Hardly a tutoring session goes by when Lily does not receive a package with high-priced clothing. Her housekeeper, Ruby, a no-nonsense woman from Barbados who is studying for her college degree, is kept busy toting in packages from J.Crew and Splendid that seem to make Lily momentarily very happy in between writing papers and studying for math tests with her corps of tutors in nearly every subject. Lily is a slightly plump girl with blond hair, pale skin, and blue eyes. Her mother is petite and thin, and she says out loud that she hopes "squash will allow Lily to lose her baby fat." Her mother keeps a precise calendar so that her daughter's tutoring appointments are neatly staggered.

In the midst of tutoring sessions, Lily rips open boxes with abandon to reveal outfits that seem far too tropical to wear in February in New York City. They also seem far too daring to wear to school—such as the leopard-print jumpsuit whose arm holes plummet well past her pink bra. She gets her own budget and picks out her own clothing. She favors Comme des Garçons, and I briefly fall in love with the high-top canvas sneakers and mariner shirts with hearts on them until I discover that the shoes cost upward of $135 (many cost several hundreds of dollars) and a simple cotton T-shirt costs more than $150. That means that one hour of tutoring would not pay for that shirt plus taxes. I quickly get used to having cheaper clothing than most of the kids I teach and tutor. One unkind seventh-grade girl whose clothes are far nicer than mine asks me, "Where did you get *that* vest?" It was a vest I think I had bought in one of those secondhand stores, definitely not the chic kind where Prince bought his raspberry beret, and though I'm not proud to admit it, I never wore it again.

Clothes are often a bargaining chip for Lily. By age sixteen, she already has a signature style, and clothes are used as a reward. An only child, she often isn't happy with her parents' constant business trips, and they allow Lily to raid her mother's closet to keep her from complaining too much. Her parents return home from Paris or Tokyo with expensive clothes. Days off with her mom, a busy executive, are often spent shopping, as that's how her mom relaxes. Lily and her mom head to Madison Avenue and then stop for a gelato or pastry at Sant Ambroeus, the New York branch of a Milanese pasticceria. (There's also a summer branch in Southampton on Long Island.)

Lily's mom, Lisa, only shares my name with her besties, the women she sweats in Pilates with, and I am flattered that the moms think I'm a kind of tutoring messiah. Other than my grandmother, no one has ever endowed me with that kind of power before. Of course, there is the Fifth Avenue mother who almost doesn't hire me when I ask her, "Which side of Fifth Avenue do you live on?" She pauses for a menacingly long time and replies acidly, "There is only one side." I hadn't recalled that one side of Fifth Avenue is the entry to Central Park in the prime residential areas uptown. I lacerate myself about that out-of-towner mistake for the better part of a month, but I still get the gig.

Getting tutoring gigs is more than just a lark to me. It is not just about my credentials or the reality that I can speak about most novels and eras of history with my eyes shut. I'll remember the year of the reunification of Germany long after I am hauled off to assisted living. That's just the way my mind works. But for me, tutoring means the difference between being able to pay for my son's babysitter or not. It means finally being able to cross my legs without showing the holes in my shoes.

Because so many private-school kids must endure college-level classes taught by PhDs who don't believe in offering extra help, the tutoring industry in Manhattan and parts of

Brooklyn is incredibly robust. The pay is what the market demands. There are tutors who charge several hundreds of dollars per hour. SAT and ACT tutors are in their own league. Several companies jumped into this Wild West years ago with prices that start at $300 and go up to $800—*per hour*. For this price, they had better come up with results. I charge $125–$175 per hour (though I have a sliding scale for families with need, and I've volunteered my time to tutor for organizations that help underprivileged kids get private-school or equivalent educations), and I never go up on my rates, though many people tell me I should. No matter the rate, sometimes it's hard to get families to pay their invoices, even people who have Hamptons houses (the Hamptons comprise the dazzlingly expensive resort area at the end of Long Island where I couldn't afford to eat lunch, much less to stay) and send their kids to $50,000-a-year private schools without any financial aid. Even if they agree to pay this amount, they don't actually pay when the bill comes. Most do, but there are always one or two holdouts. There was one mother who didn't pay me for months. Meanwhile, I saw pictures of her in glossy magazines appearing at society events. My accountant told me to write off my bill, but the Taurean-stubborn streak in me made me call this überrich mother every day for two weeks until the check for $600—then a great deal of money to me—showed up in my mailbox, written from her private wealth-management account. Other parents take a long time to pay because accountants handle every payment they make, and they actually can't write any checks—or so they say.

Other parents never mention money. When I speak to

them about my services, they don't even ask my fee. It's astounding. I feel worried, not knowing when or how I should bring it up, so I usually send them a follow-up email telling them what it is. It is amazing that money isn't something they talk about. They seem oblivious to it, just as when they ask me whether I'll be in the Hamptons over the summer. This type of question shows no awareness of what average people earn and what things cost. Some of the parents have inherited money, but some work for it. Surely they must realize their children's teachers earn well under $100,000, unless they have been teaching for a very long time. Though this sounds like a lot on a national scale, in New York City it does not cover much. It barely pays the rent on a basic two-bedroom apartment and the cost of living, unless one is fortunate enough to have bought an apartment years before the gentrification of many New York neighborhoods.

One mother, looking at my black boots, asks me, "Prada?"

"Banana Republic," I reply, wondering how she could think that I could afford $800 pairs of shoes. The Banana Republic I went to was at an outlet mall in Massachusetts where shoes cost less than a taxi ride from Brooklyn to Manhattan.

At first, I half-heartedly try to play the game of looking like I shop in the same stores as the New York City 1 percent. I have one pair of nice flats that I bought at deep discount, and I try to wear black garments that are so amorphous as to seem expensive—or at least elusive. Over time, as I move to Brooklyn and teach among children who wear leather pants in elementary school and who can peg a Fendi bag at a distance, I realize that I wasn't marinated in the juices of fashion as a youngster and have little to no chance of developing a sense of New York taste. I've never mastered the art of wearing clothes ironically, as real New Yorkers do, such as cutting Gucci pants into shorts or looking good in mom jeans paired with a short T-shirt. My idea of dressing is still to wear a semi-ironed button-down shirt with khakis—a style that I call Formal Teacher.

When I shop in the boutiques that line Court Street in Brooklyn, I simply become flummoxed. I really don't understand what the garments are or how one is supposed to wear them. As someone on a fixed budget and who works with children, I don't understand how to build a wardrobe out of $350 midi-revealing camisoles, and I only learn about Catherine Malandrino when a fashionable student at an all-boys' school I work at gives a presentation about his internship there. "Women all love Malandrino's details," I recall him saying, as the rest of the class and I wondered what he was talking about. Over time, as I give up stylish boots in favor of shapeless flats, parents stop mistaking my shoes for Prada. I decide to send the parents the signal that I'm not of their world. There are some private-school teachers who mysteriously look the part of fashionistas, which confused me until I discovered that trust funds paid their credit-card bills.

Some parents get it. They understand that New York City teachers, without a trust fund, must skirt the rim of Manhattan and Brooklyn Heights life, looking in. One Upper East Side mother, originally from the South, orders dinner for me every time I tutor her son in the SAT. When I am on my way back home to Brooklyn, she hands me a bag with a roast chicken, potatoes, vegetables, and biscuits. "You're looking after my son, and I'm looking after you," she tells me in her Tennessee twang. Sometimes there is even a piece of chocolate layer cake (with a side of whipped cream). She apologizes for not having cooked the meal herself. Her warmth makes me positively glow. Other parents forget to even offer me a cup of water. One Brooklyn Heights mother has her son's snack waiting for him as soon as he gets home. Usually, it is something mouthwatering like a turkey wrap and a cold glass of chocolate milk. She places it before him—or the nanny does when she isn't there—on a china plate with a cloth napkin. She never once asks me if I would like something, even a drink. It isn't surprising that it takes her a long time to pay my invoices.

My access to this world is through my job. Working as a learning specialist at an elite private school, I get to know evaluators, psychologists who assess students to see if they have learning differences. They come to like me, and they refer new students to me. They sometimes send so many students to me that I feel panicked from the pressure. There is simply not enough time in my day, given my full-time job and my son and husband, for me to take on all the students who need help from a learning specialist. I work six days a week, including most of the day on Sunday, and I still have parents and evaluators begging me to find time in my schedule for new students.

But I am careful never to take on more than I can handle. I devote myself assiduously to each child and their family. That means endless calls with parents, therapists, other tutors, and teachers—none of which I charge for. I spend lots of mental time mulling over each child, replaying what they've said and what they have coming up, and I search my mind for new strategies to help them do better.

One of the most critical tools I can use in my trade is metaphors. I have to put the whole game of learning into terms that the students can understand. The problem is that their education and its goals have been framed for them by other people who have their own goals—including parents who want their kids to be academic superstars and teachers who want the kids to be on the level of graduate students in eighth grade. Instead, their worlds must be reframed in accordance with their own internal guideposts. With a student athlete, such as Trevor, school has to be recast as preparing for a soccer game, and with Lily, who is tentative and feels her inferiority at each moment of the day, school must be recast as a series of controllable steps, each of which she can handle.

The problem is that I'm often playing this game with the kids without full knowledge of everything going on in their lives. Though some families are completely aboveboard with me, others keep the essential pieces of the puzzle hidden.

Ben's family in particular moved through a world I can hardly fathom. He was a boy who lived with his family in a luxury hotel, and his parents were never home. It was only from Googling on the internet, still patchy in those early days, that I found out that his father was under investigation by the SEC and that his mother's European banking family had cut her off financially. I saw a therapist's card and an allergist's card on his hotel desk, so I gathered that he was getting help for his apparent depression and his wheezing, but his mother doesn't tell me any of this because I never meet her face-to-face—not even once.

Still, the puzzle is in part what intrigues me. Kids are a kaleidoscope of intellectual interests, abilities, and moods, and every time I meet with one, such as Ben, I find a new piece of glass that pops out from the ever-shifting patterns. Though he was generally lethargic about his reading, for example, Ben surprised me by liking Faulkner's *As I Lay Dying,* about a family, colored by Southern gothic tradition, trying to bury their mother. "What a crazy family," he said grinning, as if relieved that the fictional Faulknerian Bundrens from rural Mississippi were nuttier than his Manhattan family.

These kids are not my kids, and I don't think of them that way. But I think of them as friends, as younger siblings perhaps, and I feel that I can change their lives just a bit, as they can change mine. There is little I hope to replicate about their upbringings for my own son, nor could I attempt to, given my different income bracket, but I feel that I can contribute a great deal to them in the span of one or two hours a week. I start with a two-minute warm-up, and we move into the work. In the span of about fifty minutes, I can give them enthusiastic background context about the work they are reading or the history they are studying, dive into the work, and remind them of the skills they are using.

These hours, to me, are often more exciting than the time I spend at my job working at the school, where I meet with students but also must complete endless applications to the College Board and ACT to get accommodations for students on standardized tests. On the other hand, what I like about my job at this private school is that I get to meet the types of kids I wouldn't be able to meet as a tutor—kids who are on scholarships and whose parents would never be able to pay for outside help (I offer a sliding scale, but some private schoolers are on complete scholarship, and their parents cannot afford tutoring at any price). There is, for example, Ansel, the kid whose father is an artist and who lives in a studio apartment in Harlem. Going to private school means he has to spend his days with peers he doesn't necessarily relate to, but his presence allows me to connect with other types of kids. However, there is little time in the context of a school day to do the kinds of in-depth learning-specialist work I can do in private practice.

Working in a private school can also be somewhat destabilizing, at least when you're young. One private school where I worked for a time is exclusive, accepting only a small fraction of the seemingly endless students who apply. Many of the teachers make it clear that I am not a member of their scholarly club. Some seem to have personality disorders that make them divide the world into those who pass muster and those who don't. I am hazed by some of the teachers for the first year, when the students, parents, and teachers test me out to see if I can hack it.

One of the rites of passage at my school is parents shunning the new faculty until we prove ourselves. When a letter to a student's family, written by the previous person in my job, has the wrong name on it, the mother leaves a screed on my answering machine. "You clearly don't care about my son!" she roars into her phone. My knees shake as I listen to it. Another mother asks me to call her immediately, and when I do, she asks me to call back in ten minutes. I often feel as though I'm in a hall of fun-house mirrors. When it is clear that I can survive after the first year, mainly because getting up with my son in the middle of the night makes me sleep deprived and I don't notice much around me, the teachers warm up to me a bit.

There are many lovely families at the school. There are others who scream at me and leave vituperative messages on my voice mail. I'm sure it is partly because I am young. I have a kind of round face that makes me look younger than I am, so even in my early thirties, I do not command much gravitas. I feel alone much of the time at work and sense that the situation with families at my school is often adversarial when I don't want it to be.

However, the families I tutor for are closer to me. They regard me as their savior, some of them. Though I realize this isn't emotionally healthy, it feels good to be welcomed, to be respected and admired. One set of parents whose child I tutor even says, "Your school is lucky to have you!" while I feel that isn't necessarily the opinion of everyone at the school—not because I don't work hard or care but because there is constant tension with the families. I am not in my home state of Massachusetts, and I can't get home that often, given the school schedule. When I'm in other people's warm houses, I think of my own parents' house near Boston. Tutoring comes to be the way I feel wanted and welcomed in what has to be one of the most unwelcoming cities in the world.

But getting tutoring jobs to pay my rent is about far more than just being intimate with the details of German reuni-

fication. More critically, I have to learn the ways of Fretful on Fifth Avenue, my fond term for the anxious strivers
who live in Upper East Side luxury buildings. One psychologist who makes a lot of money evaluating Upper East
Side students for learning disabilities looks at my credentials
(Harvard Phi Beta Kappa and doctoral degree in psychology from Rutgers), and we have a long talk about education, learning differences, and private schools. At the end
of the conversation she says, "And you're pretty, too," implying that a person who only attended Harvard and has a
doctoral degree in psychology isn't enough. I am entering a
world where fat is stopped at the door, where people don't
seem to have bad hair days, and where even teachers wear
Delman flats. Being untouched by acne seems equally important in this world to having read all of George Eliot's
works. Fortunately, acne is the one problem I never had,
and this evaluator *kvells* over me and starts recommending
me as a tutor to families on Fifth and Park.

Once I enter the lives of people on Fifth Avenue, I no
longer wonder about the evaluator's assessment of me. She
is only being realistic about what flies in this world—and
what doesn't.

Trevor's family refers me to their cousin Julia. One afternoon, after having tutored her for several weeks, I enter the
living room of her grand Fifth Avenue duplex to find her
mother, whom I've never met, uncharacteristically present.
She welcomes me warmly, and I am about to speak with her
about Julia before photographers descend and welcome me
to the shoot. The apartment's Christmas setup is going to
be featured in a national shelter magazine, and once I make

it clear that I am not part of the shoot, I am quickly ushered upstairs to Julia's room. She, used to her mother's exposure in magazines, is blasé about the whole thing.

But there is more to tutoring than just earning enough money to live, though it's addicting to live in a world in which a bill of $2,000 a month usually gets paid without delay. Entering this world means being vicariously connected to a life of seeming ease and beauty when my own life is rushed and panicky. There are many nights when I can't sleep because I'm worried about money, and on most days, I work full-time and then rush to the subway to head to tutoring and then rush home to pick up my son at daycare. And I don't allow myself to call in sick often because I don't want to miss out on money or disappoint the students I work with.

One early spring day, I am invited by a mother at one of the schools where I teach to be the guest at a Park Avenue women's book-club meeting. It meets at one in the afternoon, an hour that is convenient for women who don't work but for no one else. As I steal away from my school in the early afternoon, taking the Seventy-Ninth Street crosstown bus at a magic hour when it glides across Central Park with no traffic, I marvel at the time I've lost by staying inside my school rather than strolling around New York.

The hostess of the book club has just moved from DC to New York; her husband is transitioning from government to banking, and she looks more wool-suit-from-inside-the-Beltway than she does Upper East Side. She wears a navy suit, pearls, and kitten heels with a blond hairdo that comes dangerously close to being a mullet with highlights. I can tell from her address, which is on Eighty-Sixth Street but not on one of the Avenues, that she had to find housing quickly. She'll move to a more prestigious address on Fifth or Park before the year is out, I have no doubt. In the meantime, she is doing her best to fit in with the other Upper East Side women by joining this book club; I admire her moxie. The other women are more prototypically New York. One woman wears the most ornate pair of stockings I've ever seen—silk decorated with embroidered flowers that retail for over $300. (There are stores on the Upper East Side that just sell hosiery, which is not something I've worn since my wedding day.) The women are so thin that I wonder how they can manage to keep their intestines inside their bodies. As someone who turns to pizza when life gets complicated, I marvel at their ability to stay reedlike while having children and living in a city with Zabar's and Italian pastry.

After the women mill about drinking tea in porcelain cups and saucers and ignoring the canapés, I am invited to speak about one of the books I've written on study skills and ADHD, and the women pepper me with questions about their children and private-school teachers. They can spend a lot of time microanalyzing their children's lives and even preparing for what lies ahead. Their children are in lower (as private schools call elementary schools, in the British fashion) or middle school, but these mothers are eager to know what is coming. Unlike these stay-at-home moms, I can only plan for a few months at a time, as the daily grind of working full-time and tutoring doesn't leave that much more mental space.

"What are the tests like in high school at your school?" they want to know. It's clear none of them have actually read my book, which is about strategies to prepare for different types of tests and papers. They really just want the insider's guide to my Manhattan private school.

"There are grueling midterms," I tell them. "Kids have to write several essays about history, and they write on long novels in a way that requires both analysis and recall of plot details."

"Do kids really take science classes over the summer before they take them at school?" another mother wants to know.

"Yes, some kids are doing that. It's happening more and more," I say. "That's the way kids find that they can do well and not get outperformed by other kids who've taken summer classes."

The mothers gasp or cluck at several points during my talk, and I feel them joining me in a kind of alliance. Some of the women sit around the floor in a circle, their legs folded neatly underneath them. We are all together in this, my words suggest, and we'll get your kids through these insane private schools. Suddenly, my simple Target dress, the hem coming down, and the reality that I forgot to shave my bare legs don't matter that much anymore. I've been sucking in my belly for the better part of an hour—ever since childhood I've had the kind of belly that is the opposite of a six-pack—but I let the air in it release. They like me here, messy hair notwithstanding.

I've never met such a well-turned-out group before. I'm amazed that people can spend their afternoons in such pleasant ways—talking about books, drinking Mariage Frères tea, and feeling totally unrushed for time. The women even try to find some common ground with me. When they ask me where I live, the hostess stammers to her housekeeper, "Charlie had a baseball game in Brooklyn the other day. Where was it?"

After conferring with the housekeeper, the hostess is still unable to tell me exactly where her son's game was, and I'm not sure whether it was Flatbush, Red Hook, or somewhere in between. Nonetheless, it was the hostess's attempt at interborough solidarity. She might just have said, "I've heard of Brooklyn" and left it at that. The mothers are incredibly polite, though they leave off speaking about my book after about fifteen minutes and instead talk at length about their children, their teachers, and activities. It is from them I learn that children can go to space camp.

When I leave, the women give me a John Derian decoupage tray with butterflies that sells for close to $400. I use it to hold my bills on my desk at home, and I enjoy looking at it until it is overwhelmed with paper and no longer visible beneath the stack of paper.

After this tea, I become adept at spotting private-school mothers on the subway with their children. This is rare, as many of them take cabs and private cars across the city and eschew public transportation. They are noticeable by their fine clothes, nearly uniform look of skinny, unblemished blondness (with a few brunettes tossed in for good measure), and bodies toned from endless Pilates. Rushing to tutoring or home, I enjoy listening in on their conversations.

On one long Tuesday, when I leave home at 7:00 a.m. and

have a ninety-minute faculty meeting after school, I wedge myself into a small spot on the subway with my umbrella and look nervously at my phone, hoping I can get home in time to relieve my son's babysitter. Nearby, there is a mother wearing a mididress with cap sleeves and a plunging V-neck that shows off her Tree of Life necklace studded with diamonds and sapphires. Beside her sits a girl of about eight, her blond hair in French braids.

"Camilla, would you like to buy a dress for the end-of-the-year concert?" The daughter nods. "You'll look so pretty!" the mother tells her.

"Can I have another dress for Madison's wedding?" the child wants to know.

"Of course, silly," her mother responds. "A school dress isn't for weddings. That's a different kind of dress." Her words make me think about the way, when I was eight, I wore the same Gunne Sax dress to every occasion as long as it fit—everything from relatives' bat mitzvahs to birthday parties to warm days when I had nothing else to wear to school.

I imagine this woman, dressed in heels and a cashmere sweater, taking her daughter to an expensive Upper East Side children's clothing boutique where, amid the glass cases with perfectly folded white baby clothes, there are floral dresses with fitted bodices and sashes that can be tied into bows. On the day of the concert, the little girl will wear glittery flats from Crewcuts, J.Crew's pricey children's line, with a matching kid-size clutch, also covered in glitter. I order most of my son's clothes on the internet in bulk and only in solids or stripes, and I envy the mother's ability to think for so long about one dress. I'm sure on the day of the concert, her daughter's French braids will look perfect, while I congratulate myself on being able to pass a comb through my son's hair when I can. I simply can't keep up with these type of people. I just enjoy observing them.

I am intrigued by the way in which the parents on Park supercharge every moment of their child's life with purpose and drive. I spent most of my childhood feeding guppies and letting my fickle cats in and out of the house. On other days, I played in the crater that glacial activity had carved in our snowy yard and was babysat by the Estonian family next door. I had a fairly laid-back upbringing because it was the 1970s, and we were all just worried about heating our house in the oil crisis and learning the metric system that President Carter was imposing on us. Though my parents were Jews from Brooklyn, very few people where I grew up had even been to New York City. The intensity of the city was far away from our silent, snowbound world, and even nearby Boston was then a decaying city partially overshadowed by the braininess of Cambridge. If we had grown up on Fifth Avenue rather than in rural Massachusetts, my parents would have made sure my twin brother and I had learned Estonian from our neighbors. (Imagine putting that you speak Estonian on your college application!) We only learned the word for *bear* in the five years the neighbors watched us. The only words I could pick out in their rapid-fire speech were our names. We did watch some Estonian folk dances and many episodes of the 1970s gothic soap opera *Dark Shadows*. My parents, who worked in Boston as lawyers, left us alone to eat Breyers ice cream and learn about liberal politics by watching reruns of *All in the Family*. My days were just days.

But the way in which these parents care about their kids' grades and the importance they attach to me as a tutor are energizing and attractive. The parents often vet me at great lengths in their living rooms before agreeing to hire me. Some even have their assistants arrange interviews with me, and they interview a host of other tutors before settling on one. I become accustomed to entering these gladiator-style contests, often showing up to the family's apartment when the other contestants are being ushered out. For these interviews during cold-weather months, I wear the shearling coat my parents bought wholesale for me—the only respectable piece of cold-weather clothing I own. During one warm-weather interview, I am forced to don my one little black dress from Target. I wear it with a cardigan and pretend that I wear black dresses every day. Of course, my flats have holes.

The grueling interview before being hired includes showing my résumé, answering questions about which schools I've tutored at, and stating whether I've specifically tutored at that child's school. After tutoring for a number of years, I've read most every book that high-school and college students read and have memorized most of them, including *To Kill a Mockingbird, Romeo and Juliet,* The *Odyssey, The Catcher in the Rye, A Raisin in the Sun, Pride and Prejudice, Of Mice and Men, Huckleberry Finn, Hamlet,* and of course, *The Great Gatsby*, but it's still necessary to answer questions on this score. I don't really mind this vetting. There is hardly a question I can't answer, hardly a course I haven't tutored for, and I have my elevator pitch down to a science.

During one memorable meet and greet with parents at a Manhattan café, I wait nervously for the couple until I spot a man with a five-o'clock shadow wearing cigarette pants, loafers without socks, and a pink pocket square. I pray to a nameless god that he isn't the father of the prospective student, but, indeed he is. Let's call this man Don Draper, as he reminds me of the protagonist from *Mad Men*. The blond wife is flawlessly beautiful and thin as a reed (Betty Draper!), and I wonder how she maintains this figure after having four children until I find out she works out with her personal trainer each morning and is incommunicado until about noon.

In between trying to take sips of my green tea, I have to answer questions from Don Draper such as, "Have you read the books on my son's syllabus?" I have, some so often that I could point students to passages without cracking the spine of the book.

They grill me about other students I've worked with. "Did their grades go up?" they want to know. (*No, their grades did not always improve when kids didn't work hard enough,* I explain. *But, if they did the work, they usually improved. I can't offer a magic bullet.* Not a good answer, I can tell from the frowns on their faces.)

"Do you know the teachers at my son's school?" (*Yes, I had met with several of them and had spoken to them on the phone countless times.* Don Draper and wife disagree with me that their son's teachers are amazing educators, but they hire me anyway, perhaps because I have already tutored several kids from their son's school.)

Then there is often the personal meet and greet with the child to see if the *chemistry* (this is the word the parents most often use) is good. I leave these meetings feeling animated, ready to crack the code of each kid and figure out how to excite them about academics. I have my series of go-to jokes, which largely allows me to make fun of myself for several minutes and to josh about how much fun the student and I are going to have working on reading *The Odyssey* over the summer or learning every tariff in American history.

When I first meet Lily in the summer before her freshman year of high school, I get a smile out of her by telling her how much fun we're going to have previewing *The Great Gatsby* over the summer. "I'm sure there is nothing you'd rather do," I say, and she smiles, tears glittering in the corners of her anxious eyes. This is one of the tricks of my trade—helping kids by giving them an introduction to the complicated works they'll read ahead of time. This helps them absorb some of the context of the book, and it's a way to work around the difficulty some kids with language-processing issues have absorbing large quantities of complicated text in quick order. The kids like my sarcastic comments, which show that I know that their schoolwork is dull for them. There are only a few kids among dozens who remain harder for me to crack than the Enigma code was for Turing.

Then there is the phase when we move into scheduling. This can be quite taxing, as kids have schedules that are very cluttered. Most have after-school sports and travel teams, and they go away often. Scheduling for Lily was well-nigh impossible because of her squash lessons and tournaments, not to mention her weekends in the Hamptons.

"Lily just adores you," her mother tells me in a phone call after we've met for the first time. "We'd love to work with you."

"Well, thanks," I tell her.

"So, her math tutor comes on Mondays and Fridays at five. Any chance you could come at six?"

Friday afternoon is my sacred time—not religious time, but time to see my son right after work. It's the only weekday he doesn't have a babysitter.

"No, I can't do that," I tell her.

"Oh, no chance of 6:00 p.m. on Fridays?" she replies, sounding surprised. "Would seven on Fridays work?"

"I don't tutor on Fridays," I tell her.

"How about Saturday morning at ten?" she asks me. This is the other time in the week when I'm unwilling to work. "Sometimes we're in the Hamptons, but we can start with that time and shift during the spring."

"Sorry, also not good," I say, wondering how Lily's mother expects me to shift my schedule each week when she decides to go to the Hamptons. "How about any day of the week before five?"

"Oh dear," she frets. "And Lily liked you so much. Well, she has her personal trainer on Wednesdays at four, so that's out."

"That would be a good time for tutoring," I say.

"We can't move her personal trainer. It's important for her cross-training for squash."

"Okay," I say. "It's either then or Thursday at four."

"No, that's also impossible. Her squash lessons start at five thirty on that day, and our housekeeper has to get her to Brooklyn Heights."

"Well, that would be a good time," I tell her.

"All right. I'll see if Ruby can give Lily dinner beforehand, and they can Uber over there to Brooklyn. It'll be a mad rush, but since she liked you so much, we'll try to make it work."

That's how I wind up wedged into Lily's schedule in between school and sports practice and why she's always eating sushi, trying to fit in dinner, while we're tutoring. She munches on California rolls and spicy tuna rolls, tearing bits of seaweed off with her teeth while we're trying to read *Julius Caesar* together. As a result, the smell of soy sauce always reminds me of Shakespeare.

Parents are loath to give up any of these activities, yet I am yelled at when I miss a tutoring appointment that I am not sure the kid has committed to keeping. (It is during a snowstorm, and I've decided to head home to Brooklyn.) The mom is clearly bummed out. "But I canceled a violin lesson for you," she wails, as if her son's one-hour stagnation will result in ruin.

Though stagnation is as rare as flab on Fifth Avenue, it is actually these short periods of seeming stagnation that can really benefit kids. The research has been robust on this point, but no matter how many times I preach the benefits of relaxing, parents look at me like I'm an antiquated freak. Kids need to turn off their minds, much like switching off

the screens on their computers, if they hope to be productive during other points of the day. They need downtime
to consolidate their thoughts and to let their mind come up
with other solutions. The mind works during these turned-
off times; it's the reason that the best thoughts come to you
in the shower or when you're doing the dishes. Your brain
is relaxed, at rest, and your free-flowing association net-
work is more active. If children's lives are constantly struc-
tured, they don't know how to cope with boredom or being
alone. Their minds are primed for constant feedback from
others or from electronics, and the moments in which they
can come to know themselves, their dreams, their flash
points, and their epiphanies have been stolen from them,
never to return. It is especially during childhood, when
one is fleshing out one's values, that these moments are so
magical, but the kids I work with don't seem to be able to
fit them into their day.

Lily is an example of a kid whose life does not permit her
any moments of flow, a concept developed by Hungarian-
American psychologist Mihaly Csikszentmihalyi to refer to
states of productive absorption in one's work. In this state,
people are at peace and so absorbed in their work that they
don't notice time passing. Flow leads to happiness and an
intense belief in one's own abilities. It is a state that parents
should want children to experience, but the culture of modern childhood has stolen these moments from many kids.

Lily goes from squash practice at dawn to a grueling private-school schedule to more squash practice after school to
homework and tutors. Squash is more than an arcane racket
sport. For Lily, squash is about far more than what happens

on the court. It is a ticket to a prestigious college, such as one in the Ivy League or an elite liberal-arts school, where squash is played avidly. She tells me that she enjoys sewing, and I see her needlework, which is precise and deft. "I'd love to be a fashion designer," she says wistfully, eyeing the opened pages of her Elle magazine, "but I don't have time to take the fashion classes I want to." The one time I see her sewing, Lily seems to be at total peace, handy with a needle, sure with her stitches, and this is a world in which she could relax and find solace. She is more at home with a needle than with a squash racket, but she is not permitted to drop one piece of equipment for the other.

When I work with these kids, I let them talk for a little bit, make a few jokes. It might be the first break they've had all day, and they are usually grateful for a dose of levity. It's a lot to have squash practice before school, a whole day of intense academics, squash practice after school, and two tutors after school—one to help you structure your essay on *Lolita* (I don't help kids write the essays, but I do help them organize their own thoughts), and a later one to work on the SAT. I'm just one stop in their never-ending cycle, but I might as well make it an amusing one. That means I'm willing to take detours into everything adolescent. After waffling, I have to decide which member of One Direction I like best because my tutees don't accept that I have no clear preference. "Zayn," I declare with feigned confidence because all the others blend together in my mind.

Working with the kids is invigorating, and I'm touched by them. They are vulnerable. At the same time that I sympathize with them, I am in awe of their outward sophistication. They are like the teddy bears made by Prada—fluffy and cute yet also stylish. The kids have a kind of insouciant, effortlessly chic style that is outside of my price range. They tend to look kind of Frenchy, almost as if their dresses should come with a pastel-colored bike and a baguette. They also have expensive accoutrements, such as squash rackets that cost close to $200. The books they read in their private schools are enticing. I can't imagine reading *Lolita* as a high schooler. My excitement over their opportunities to write, to think, to look insouciant tides me over on my long, fluorescent-lit subway trip home to Brooklyn.

There are, however, kids who wear the privilege of Park Avenue lightly. Trevor's dad looks like he should be some kind of baron in Downton Abbey, and he has the requisite lockjaw for the part. But Trevor—freckled, Brooks Brothers shirt spilling out of his saggy jeans, armpits smelly from playing soccer, unrestrained about telling me that his teachers suck (when, in reality, he hasn't ever learned how to read well)—doesn't let his father's dark moods and mild disapproval affect him. Instead, Trevor volunteers to help the janitor power-wash the gum off the sidewalk in front of their Fifth Avenue apartment building. (That explains why Fifth Avenue doesn't have any grease or blemishes on the sidewalks: power washes.) Trevor is so buoyant he literally bounces off the sidewalk, weaving between the older women with poodles. It's his devil-may-care attitude that later convinces him that the police will never catch him committing crimes, but I don't know the dark side of his insouciance when I meet him. Instead, I'm just intrigued by how he can live with an oppressively dour father and remain so shamelessly ebullient.

His father has so much gravitas it's a minor miracle that he doesn't fall through the concrete of the New York City sidewalks. He's a man who manages to wear gray even in the summer, even on the weekends. On the weekdays, he wears a Brooks Brothers suit with a white shirt and a repp tie. His shoes are polished, and he doesn't carry an ounce of extra fat. His face has indentations where cheeks should be, and even his eyes are colorless. Being critical is his default setting.

Trevor tells me, in the only warm memory he seems to have of his father, "When I was little, my dad used to bring me to the office on Saturday mornings. He'd do his work, and I'd do mine, which meant coloring on legal pads." I wonder why Trevor had to draw on lined paper; even as a preschooler, he wasn't permitted an open canvas. He grins and has a kind of singsong quality when telling this anecdote, retrieving it from childhood memories. He manages to emerge from that experience with a sense of unbridled fun—a miracle of some proportions.

Through my association with Lily, I sometimes get to vicariously experience the lives of the fabulously wealthy. While tutoring her, I drink tea out of Rosenthal china cups with Imari patterns. I get to go to her Hamptons house. It is there that I get one of my few breaks from the heat and smell of New York City. Though one mother claims that "No one is in the city in the summer," I am, along with the rest of the working world, trying to make money.

It is in the Hamptons, where the überrich and the wannabe-rich spend the summer on Long Island, that I understand that these New Yorkers don't have to sweat unless they want to. The kids who live this life are truly "Gatsby's children," the spiritual heirs of Fitzgerald's hero, who lived in luxury in Long Island. They can have barbecues on lush lawns and dip into their pools. They can attend charity auctions and see most everyone else they know from the Upper East Side. They can read *The Odyssey* right before a tennis match. It is here that many families spend their entire summers, not returning to the city until the minute before school starts. It is here where kids (in the days before Google Docs) could claim to have "left my homework in the Hamptons," so that those students with two houses have an excuse not available to the less wealthy. Many students used that excuse on me when I was a classroom teacher, meaning that I was supposed to cut the kids with second houses some slack, while the scholarship kids were out of luck. (The less advantaged kids could have used the excuse "I left my homework at my dad's second jobsite," but they never did.)

Lily's house in the Hamptons is understated but beautiful. Imagine a vast living room of white couches with a view of a large pool. Everything is white with touches of gray. I hate clients' white chairs, as I'm afraid I'll get them dirty. Every time I stand up, I nervously inspect the chair; it won't matter how well I can parse Romantic poetry if a melted Junior Mint seeps into their priceless fabrics.

Driving out there, I pass convertible sports cars and recall how Gatsby drove through the "valley of ashes" en route from Long Island to New York City. Traveling from Brooklyn to Long Island on a promising summer morning, I feel as though I live in the valley of ashes, the soot-ridden, urban sprawl where the gas station attendant, George Wilson, lives with his cheating wife, Myrtle, in *The Great Gatsby*. Brooklyn and Queens, in parts, are still the depository of urban refuse, the eyesores that the rich of Manhattan and Long Island must pass through to get to their respective homes. I lived briefly in Queens among gas stations, car washes, 99-cent stores, warehouses, truck depots, and other places where the people live who make the life of Manhattan possible—the hospital workers, sanitation employees, nannies, teachers, and Uber drivers. Spending the day at Lily's pool reminds me that some people need only to pass through the valley of ashes momentarily on their way to something glorious and freeing. For others, it is their everyday reality.

During the summer months, it is my job to tutor kids after a day of camp or tennis, so I find myself driving to Westchester and other places during rush hour so that I can meet with them in the late afternoons. And after a two-hour breath of fresh air and a discussion of Odysseus's trip to the underworld, I am back to my own Hades—New York City in the summer. But I'm leaving a little bit richer and with a few hours' supply of fresh air in my lungs.

The brief trips to the country and the Imari teaware are not why I keep tutoring New York City's 1 percent, though. I become addicted, for reasons both healthy and not, to trying to bring order to the kids' lives in the hour slots I have with them. Most of the kids I work with have learning differences, but they have to contend with really tough curricula. I enjoy trying to neaten things, to make someone feel better (though possibly not in the most important ways) in a short period of time. It's genetic. My grandparents and other relatives used to clean my closets and clip my nails when they came to visit. My family has a genetic aversion to disorder, and I want to bring that kind of purity to the kids' minds and book bags. In my hour with them, I try to sort out their confusion, make a plan for them to do better, clean their backpacks of crumpled papers and extra sets of expensive headphones, and cheer them up, all while doing trig equations or studying for a test on the Russian Revolution. I usually feel that their mental closets are cleaner when I'm on my way out the door.

I relive my middle- and high-school years time and time again. Though I can't afford therapy (New York City therapists are notorious for not accepting insurance and charging $250 and up per hour), I free-associate and perform self-therapy in the shower. I ask myself why I work in a high school and tutor middle- and high-school kids all week. I realize that I'm trying to go back in time to rescue or comfort my anxious teenage self. When young, I had regarded the world as an intense moral playground in which bullies had to be defeated and the friendless rescued. At times, because of my internal morality play, I lacked nuance and proportion. If only I could have done it differently, I think. If only I had known that better things were on the horizon than the cruelty and closed-mindedness of other teenagers. This is what I'm trying to impart during those endless hours sitting beside kids. The money is good, and necessary, but in all those fifteen years, I do not raise my rates. I could, especially after publishing several books on learning issues and working in different private schools, but I don't. Obviously, I am getting something out of this work, just as the kids are.

2

The Pie Chart

On a sultry September afternoon that promises a torrential downpour, the teachers at the New York City private school where I work are stuffed into the overheated chapel staring up at a large screen in front. Sweat rings under his armpits, a consultant has been hired by the school to examine our progress, and he is telling us about the parents whose kids attend our school. He gets to a slide that presents the average income of the parents and shows a colorful pie chart with different slices of the income pie. I shut my eyes, not wanting to see what's there.

"So, the average income of your parents is $750,000," he says, trying to move on quickly. A collective titter runs through the teachers, a mixture of a sigh, a laugh, and a grunt. To try to get some context, I force myself to look at the pie chart. The largest slice is the one representing incomes over $500,000. There are other slices, but they are narrow, kind of like the sliver of German chocolate cake you eat while trying to diet. I feel waves of heat coming over my face, reflecting my shame of what I have become—far poorer than the people I went to college with. I first encountered the ultrarich at Harvard, but they didn't seem to represent anything that I could attain. During short visits to Manhattan during college, I realized, with a sudden infusion of embarrassment, that my flip-flops and ill-fitting Maine hoodies marked me as nonnative, and after that, I never really tried to emulate the elite.

I have always known that the parents at my school are wealthy, but I try not to think too much about it. I try to not see their suede boots and, at drop-off in the morning, their costly tandem bikes on which the younger children are perched in French sailors' shirts. If I see these things, I try not to think about their price tags, but this man's presentation is confronting me with the reality that the parents make about ten times what I do.

After the information is released, the teachers settle into a cool insouciance, as if to suggest they always knew how wealthy the parent body was. Nothing shocks them, it suggests. But I continue to feel, above all things, shame. It's interesting that I don't feel outrage that teachers aren't paid better. Instead, I feel hopelessly left behind, unable to keep up, and fearful of being exposed. I wonder if this is how the scholarship students at the school feel—like they are faking it by wearing counterfeit Ray-Bans and expensive-looking costume jewelry until someone asks them where they went for vacation and they have to admit they spent it at home on Flatbush Avenue.

There is a lot of other information in the presentation, including the way parents feel about different services at the school. By far, the most positively endorsed sector of the school—the one that parents and students like the most—is the college-counseling office. The teachers break into applause for our bright, hardworking college counselors. I do not begrudge them this popularity, but I feel sorry for the other teachers, the ones who prepare lessons every day, work with the kids at their best and their worst, and care about how much the kids learn. Collectively speaking, classroom teachers will never be the most popular asset of any private school (though some individuals might be popular) because they assign grades—and some of those grades are not good. The parents at our school value college admission, which involves a one-year process of working with the college counselors from the middle of junior year until roughly the middle of senior year (with some residual activities until the end of senior year), more than they value the rest of the twelve-year process (or longer) that gets kids to junior year.

In places like Manhattan and Brooklyn and Palo Alto, the sector of residents who count themselves in the top 1 percent is vast and includes many divisions. In the thirty-five years leading up to 2012, the income claimed by the top .01 percent quadrupled and that of the top 1 percent tripled, according to Emmanuel Saez and Gabriel Zucman at the University of California at Berkeley. To be in the top 1 percent, which received so much ire during the Occupy movement, you have to make $386,000 (in 2014), but to be in the top .01 percent, you have to pull in $1.5 million. The average income of the parents at my school puts them in the top .1–.5 percent range. Of course, these are national statistics. To be in the top 1 percent in New York, you have to make $1.55 million, and the average income in this select group of Gothamites is $8.98 million. Though these studies come from the years before COVID-19, it's clear that the pandemic has only increased the yawning gulf between haves and have-nots. Well-resourced private schools are offering robust remote programs, while many public schools offer little, or what they offer cannot be accessed by poor students without internet access or computers. The rich shelter in safe places like Wyoming and carry out their jobs remotely, sometimes hiring private teachers for their children, while many of the poor have to be exposed to the virus while working in densely packed cities.

Many of the people in the .01 percent bracket own businesses, while about one-fifth of them work in finance, including private equity and hedge funds, and they have been able to take advantage of personal tax rates charged to limited-liability corporations and S corporations rather than higher tax rates charged to regular corporations. The highest concentration of high-income households in America is in New York City, where about 12 percent of the very rich live, while 5 percent of these high-net-worth individuals live in Los Angeles.

The result is, in areas like SoHo, the Upper East Side, Brooklyn Heights, Dumbo, and other areas, a glut of people are in the stratospheric level of personal wealth. Wealth in New York City, once concentrated in Manhattan, has spread its tentacles into interesting, gentrifying neighborhoods in Brooklyn and Queens and is even beginning to appear in Staten Island and the Bronx. Now, people in neighborhoods like Crown Heights and Fort Greene live parallel lives in which hundred-dollar cognac sells next door to housing projects and twentysomething *trustafarians* drink Stumptown Coffee, living next to elderly people whose families have called these neighborhoods home for generations. One year, I saw two girls at a volleyball tryout held early in the school year talk about where they're from. "Upper East Side," says one, while the other says, "Bed-Stuy." Blond, athletic, tall, they look exactly the same. The neighborhoods are far more alike with each passing year.

The average income at my school is, of course, a flawed measure of the way many people live. Some highfliers can inflate the average, meaning that a lot of families are living at lower levels. But the fact that tuition is well over $50,000 means that many of the families are doing well, unimaginably well. While there is at least partial financial aid available for about 15 percent of the families at many New York City private schools with large endowments, most families have to be very comfortable financially to even consider sending their children to private school, unless they come through access programs that help kids from other backgrounds gain scholarships for private education. Over the twenty years leading up to 2017, the cost of private-school tuition in all states grew at a rate that outpaced inflation, putting this type of tuition well out of reach of anyone but the few who can win scholarships, the few who can cobble together some financial aid and make major sacrifices, and those who are in the 1 percent.

Many families who are wealthy by national standards also receive financial aid, in part because schools are committed to helping them once their child has been admitted. Some families also carry large financial loads from having multiple houses and many children at private schools, and schools will give financial aid to families who appear financially well-off on the surface.

In an interesting trend, rich people across the nation are having more kids than poorer people—a reversal from the last generation. In many of the families I work with, it's common to have three or four children whose unisex names sound like they are monograms from an old J.Crew catalog: Hunter, Jackson, Devin, and Tyler. As the 1 percent claim a bigger piece of the economic pie, they can also pay for more babysitting and childcare, and they can devote more resources to their children. Hence the Lincoln Navigators pulling up to private schools to drop off multiple children. Families with more than one child at a school are often more beloved by that school—they represent more tuition and a greater commitment to the institution—and children from large families are often among the most affluent.

While it was chic in the '70s to have exactly two children and for mothers to enter the workforce, it is now common-place among the rich to have large families and for women to stay at home. These women develop into übermoms who shuttle their children from sports practices to tutoring to doctor's visits, while their husbands, working in finance, dedicate themselves to the workplace.

These women are not slackers, such as I am at home. Not for them the prepared microwavable dinner or the embarrassingly dirty litter box. Not for them missing back-to-school night or failing to see a teacher's email until five days after it was sent. Not for them missing a travel-team practice or forgetting to take their child to the allergist. They devote themselves to the home, or sometimes to their many homes, and to exercise in the same way I once dedicated myself to completing grad school—it is their project, their passion, their mission. A child who doesn't do well on a test reflects poorly on these hardworking women, and their worlds are in many ways as divided by gender as the world of the 1950s. In my work, 90 percent of parents I correspond with are mothers. Every once in a while, I encounter an involved dad, but for the most part, mothers are the ones who handle their child's school life and who are expected to hire and manage tutors. These mothers are usually well educated, having attended prestigious colleges, and they take their work as parents seriously. Next to them, I do not rate. As he ages from a newborn to toddler to kindergartner, my son wears pants that are too long when the days first turn cold, in part because he refuses to go shopping and try on clothes in a store, and his hair pokes into his eyes before he gets it cut (some polite teachers at his daycare put his hair in a barrette to signify that it's time for a trim). Simple victories are all I can claim—a few sections of orange that make it past his back teeth and into his stomach, a drawing class when he is three years old, and singing lessons with a woman who doesn't speak any English but who teaches him how to breathe correctly to make his voice flow.

Like the children we work with, many teachers who work at private schools, like me, are also generally privileged. We have a great deal of education, and it is fortunate to be able to work with kids. The students at private schools are a motivated lot on the whole, and private schools are generally free of the kinds of violence that many public-school students and teachers confront. But the disparity between teacher and family incomes at private schools, particularly in New York City, is a worthwhile variable to consider in the education of children. It colors the interactions between the families and the teachers, and it colors the outlook of many, though certainly not all, of the students.

Teachers in New York City are increasingly uncomfortable because the 99 percent is hard-pressed to find housing in a borough where many two-bedroom apartments cost well over $1 million. When I first arrived in New York City in the mid-1990s, I lived in a charming Upper West Side building on a street that led to a Central Park transverse that crossed to the East Side. Lauren Bacall was my neighbor—at least down the street—and I saw the actor who played the younger brother in *The Brothers McMullen* almost every day walking around, seemingly waiting for his agent to call. Later, I had a roomy rental in a brownstone in Cobble Hill, Brooklyn, on a tree-lined street where longtime Italian residents set off fireworks on July Fourth with impunity.

Around 2007, as the cost of New York housing soared during a real-estate bubble that never really popped, my situation brought me to a two-bedroom in Brooklyn where moderately successful drug dealers lived upstairs and a man with a cauliflower ear (the result of a bar fight) was the most frequent visitor to the building. It was the kind of postwar (that is, post–Gulf War) construction that can only be described as an eyesore, with a flat brick front pocked with air conditioner sleeves.

Later, I lived in the semiheated basement rental unit of a crumbling wood-frame Brooklyn house with cold tile floors, a porch with holes large enough for a ferret to climb through, and upstairs landlords who were so in debt that they gave up their place for weeks at a time to *guests* (as they called them) who were really Airbnb customers. A visiting couple from Belgium, along with their grown-up, bespectacled son, were out for most of the day, but then some French musicians had a house party that went until 3:00 a.m., and they left the door open in a neighborhood known for gunfire. After that, I lived in Queens amid 99-cent stores, run-down hospital buildings, and massage parlors. It took me over an hour on two subways to get to my school, and many other teachers had to live far out in the periphery of the city as well. Private schools in New York City are located in the neighborhoods—the Upper East Side, the Village, Brooklyn Heights, Park Slope—where teachers can't afford to live. There was a geographic and economic gulf between the teachers and our students, and it gaped wider each year.

The teachers are often just as well educated as the parents, if not uselessly better educated, but they have chosen different careers that earn about one-seventh to one-tenth of what the parents do. In fact, the place where I've bumped into fellow Harvard alumni/ae most frequently is the admissions offices at the various private schools I've worked at. In not the most flattering moment, I think of myself as the Help—one of the people who lives downstairs in Downton Abbey—rather than as a guest at the party.

To protect their egos, private-school teachers can be a bit arrogant at times. One teacher at one school I work at constantly makes fun of the error-filled emails of parents, which is his way to feel superior in his job while trying to shop around his screenplay. Many private-school teachers send their children to the schools where they teach, as they get free or reduced tuition, and this means that they are also fellow parents. The children of the faculty are generally some of the few members of what might be called a New York City middle class, an increasingly rare group.

The income distribution at New York City private schools affects the teaching, at times. One second-grade class has to make dioramas of dinosaurs out of shoeboxes, and the kids keep showing off their T. rexes poised in Manolo Blahnik boxes. The second-graders are blissfully ignorant of what the bright brand names and logos on their shoeboxes mean (or at least, one hopes they are), and far more intrigued, rightly so, by their mastodons and pterodactyls. However, as the kids get older, it's harder to keep income out of the classroom.

As a sophomore history teacher in school, I respond to a student's question about what *conspicuous consumption* is. It is strangely hard for me to convey what it means. I keep digging for a definition that fails me because the simple one of *spending to show others how rich you are* seems axiomatic to the kids in the classroom. When I give this standard definition, they continue to stare at me, as if to say *Of course people spend so that others can see how much money they have. Duh!* I then decide to produce examples of conspicuous consumption in the gilded age. "At this time, we think of Newport, Rhode Island, and Fifth Avenue," I say, content with myself. After I use Fifth Avenue as an example of gilded-age excess, I register the look of discomfort on a student's face but do not process it. Later that same day, walking down Fifth Avenue on the way to tutor, I realize *Oh my god. Fifth Avenue isn't an icon or example to them. It's not from the past. It's where they live!* My face flushes in the wind, and I begin to realize that what I take for granted is not what they take for granted.

During the unit on labor unions in the sophomore history class I am teaching, I am particularly out of place in the classroom. While I am a privileged person, my grandparents were die-hard union members. My grandmother was a leader in 1199, the union of hospital workers, and I stupidly take it for granted that unions are universally supported in New York City. My students contradict me.

"My dad says unions are bad for business," points out one.

"Unions make things more expensive," adds another.

A new teacher, I give the students a long lecture about how poor people will take oppression only for so long, and then they revolt. Ever tenacious, I make that my overarching lesson, one that is entirely lost on most of the students no matter how many times I say it. The first time I give it, the students' faces fall, and I feel sorry for having depressed the young souls under my tutelage. Later, they give each other knowing looks, as if to say, *Dr. Grossberg is cranky today,* and then they tune out. One of my favorite students calls it the Dr. Grossberg Life-Sucks-and-Then-You-Die Speech. The other students in the class—the children of Ghanaian and Salvadoran immigrants—say nothing. When I ask them what they think, they shrug. I'm sure there's a lot more going on for them that they don't wish to bring into the classroom.

Though they may harbor certain ideas that run counter to liberalism, the parents in most New York City private schools overwhelmingly consider themselves liberal. In mock elections at the schools, in which it is presumed that children vote in similar ways to their parents, Democratic candidates overwhelmingly triumph over Republicans, similar to the results in New York City as a whole. Parents espouse liberal values in most schools, though there is a vocal minority who identify as more conservative and feel that they are not heard.

To reconcile being liberal with sending their children to private rather than public school, many parents are extremely generous to the school. In addition to giving money to help pay for financial aid for other students, they pitch themselves headlong into fundraising events. One very kind parent even paid for all the teachers at her children's school to receive free admission at the Brooklyn Museum.

Many of the parents at New York City private schools are arrivistes, people who are newly launched into the world of wealth, like the fictional Jay Gatsby, while others have been long acquainted with this world. Warren, a high-school boy

with ADHD who I tutor, is from this type of multigener-
ational wealth, tempered with a dose of SoHo bohemian-
ism. His parents attended Harvard, as did his grandfather
and generations before him. They are wealthy both from
inheritance—the grandfather bequeathed several millions
of dollars to a Harvard museum—and from the mother's
work on Wall Street. The dad is a potter, he has good
taste in art, and he has painted the walls of the family's loft
salmon. Warren's two older siblings attended Harvard, and
the question lingers in the air whether he will, too. Perhaps
because they come from a long line of privilege, Warren's
parents are uncharacteristically relaxed. When they speak
about his education, they are always concentrated on how
deeply he's thinking about the books he reads, whether he
is practicing the cello, and his upcoming exchange program
in Spain. Their kitchen table is littered with scraps of clay
and opened copies of the *New Yorker*, and they are almost
always home. When they socialize, it's not at restaurants
but at their houses. They are one of the few families I get
to know who seem to feel comfortable at home, and their
home isn't perfect but is idiosyncratic, with dying plants,
antique posters of suffragettes, and an heirloom piano.

To understand how the children on Fifth Avenue are
raised is to understand private schools. The 1 percent in
New York City almost entirely attend private schools.
Though there are some high-quality programs in special-
ized high schools spread throughout the five boroughs, including Stuyvesant, Bronx Science and the newer Brooklyn
Latin (modeled on the Boston Latin School, the oldest pub-

lic school in the US), these programs are hard to get into and are usually only at the high-school level. There are also some better public elementary schools, generally in tonier neighborhoods where parents give money to fund the PTA and pay for programs that the city can't afford. But the 1 percent, and particularly the .01 percent, gravitate to private schools. New York City is one of the areas in the country where private schools do not need to worry about their enrollments. In fact, demand greatly outstrips supply, in part because the public schools are generally crowded and lacking in resources, while there is an ample pool of parents who can and will pay over $50,000 annually for twelve (or more, starting at prekindergarten, which costs almost as much as twelfth grade) years of school for their children.

According to a report written by Sean Reardon of Stanford and Harvard Graduate School of Education professor Richard Murnane, along with doctoral students Preeya P. Mbekeani and Anne Lamb, the cost of private school has gone up about fivefold over the last few decades while middle-class incomes have flatlined. That means that the middle class finds it harder to afford any type of private education, even religious schools, which tend to cost less than some nonsectarian schools. With the falloff of attendance at private Catholic schools over the last several decades, which once catered to middle-income students, the students at private schools are increasingly from one class: the very affluent. These pools of privilege create what Reardon refers to as an "empathy gap" among affluent children for members of other socioeconomic classes. As the researchers point out, income inequality and racial inequality go hand in hand,

and affluent children are often educated without a great deal of interaction with members of other socioeconomic and racial groups. Private schools, even while they try to dispense financial aid to attract a more diverse student body, are still the domain of the wealthy—and the white.

The interactions between New York City private-school parents and the teachers and administrators at those schools are not characteristic of most public schools. While private-school parents in the old days might have dropped their kids off at the front door, shook the headmaster's hand, and let it go at that, today's NYC private-school parents want a lot of face time and interaction with their children's teachers. On many occasions, I've sat at Brooklyn and Manhattan cafés near the schools where I taught or tutored kids and heard the parents discussing their children's teachers in very thorough terms. They expend a lot of energy thinking about the teachers and analyzing which would be best for their children.

Over the years, I get to know the parents in the .01 percent in ways that go beyond the numbers. Parents, teachers, and administrators at private schools spend a lot of time speaking. As a learning specialist in this setting, I've often received emails or calls from the same parents on a daily or weekly basis. I've spent hours meeting with parents. This is not the world of ten-minute yearly conferences that might be offered at many large, urban public schools.

The parents see the private schools as part of their social scene. At one school I worked at, the parents sat in the dining hall after drop-off time and had coffee for the better part of an hour. At other New York City schools, there are nearby cafés where parents, mainly mothers, gather after drop-off to chat. Here is where, going to get a midmorning latte, I can hear them speak about teachers and kids at the school where I teach.

"Ms. Pringle is not the kind of teacher Ms. Latham was," says one mother. "She doesn't seem to get my Lexi."

"And do you think the Lenape project was fair?" asks the other mother, in between dainty bites of a green-tea muffin. "She didn't tell us about it until the day before it was due, and we barely had time to go out and get the poster board and the clay we needed."

"Ms. Latham was really good about that. The homework was in the folder the week before, so I knew what to do."

"Absolutely. I was at my book group that night—the night before the Lenape project was due—so I had to get home at nine thirty at night and start shaping clay into the longhouses, and Hunter was tearing up his soccer socks to make breechcloths. I think I'm going to be bad and have another muffin."

The parents like to know exactly what's going on at their children's school and to involve themselves in their kids' projects, and there are numerous chances for them to do so. They can call their child's adviser—the faculty member who is responsible for overseeing a student's academics and extracurriculars and well-being—as often as they would like. There are also coffees, potlucks, fundraisers, festivals, multiple conference days, and volunteer opportunities in the school. Parents have been known to leave a parents' association meeting or volleyball game and wander by the room of the teacher who has been giving their child poor grades on assignments. Once, I returned from a meeting to find the father of a student I was working with on the sofa in my office, but he did not have an appointment. He had been meeting with another teacher and had popped by my office and waited for me.

Though this type of impromptu appointment is generally frowned upon, New York City private schools provide a great deal of customer service to their parents. If, for example, a child is going to receive what is considered a poor grade—which means a grade below a B−, generally speaking—the teacher has to pave the way by giving the parents a great deal of advance notice and providing the student with ample opportunities to improve. This is a fair practice in many ways, as the teacher is not allowed to spring a poor grade on a student, but it has also enabled many parents to fight a C or a lower grade because they were not given advance warning.

These parents have the wherewithal and interest to absorb themselves intimately in their children's learning. They master the lingo of education and attend workshops on how to help their kids learn. When they sit down at conferences with their child's teachers, they can easily speak for an hour about the student's learning profile. One mother, for example, surprises me at a conference by stating, "My daughter is far better at decoding than encoding." She knows the intricacies of the process of learning to read, and she is not alone. Many of the parents hire evaluators to assess their children's learning style and to produce reports that cost upward of $4,000, a fee that insurance doesn't usually cover.

Private-school parents analyze most of the decisions their

children make and do so carefully. It's a long way from the days when I brought home a mimeographed sheet so my parents could check off whether I was taking Spanish or French. Instead, today, parents consider in detail which language is a better fit for their child, and there is a series of conversations—with the child's teachers, evaluator, and others, before the decision is made. Many private schools also offer Mandarin and Latin, and these languages are considered before parents make a final decision. Parents weigh whether languages like Mandarin will permit their children to have future business opportunities, while the reality is that few American high-school students manage to be proficient enough in Chinese to even order pork buns in Beijing, never mind conduct a business deal.

Each year, the parents weigh in on which classes their children take—and at which level. Some push for accelerated classes or AP classes (though some private schools have jettisoned the AP courses because they realize it binds them to a certain curriculum and they desire the freedom to teach what they want). They often meet with teachers in the spring to discuss the choices their children will make in the fall, and they also start the school year with conferences with their child's adviser, teachers, and coaches. Parents email their child's adviser over everything from minute details such as a missing book to larger details such as a child's difficulty with a teacher, and some parents are in daily contact with teachers. The relationship is often one of respect, sometimes one marked by conflict, and too often one in which parents exercise their power over the teacher by going to administrators.

A parent who does not like the grade their child has received often leapfrogs the teacher and goes straight to an administrator. This happens to me when I teach history. A boy who has received Bs before, though rarely, writes a paper that is off-topic, and though he is very analytical and somewhat hardworking, I have to give him a B on the merits of the paper. The parent does not approach me directly, but an administrator does, telling me that the mother called her and said, "My son has never received a B before on a paper." After I quickly do some research on the school's database, I realize that this is patently untrue, but the administrator reads me a series of remarks from her conversation with the parent, which she had transcribed nearly verbatim on loose-leaf paper, and she asks me—no, directs me—to reread the paper. I do so, fervently hoping that I can find a reason to up the grade. At the end of my reading, however, this student's work seems as off-topic as ever, and the grade feels, if anything, a bit too high to justify. I keep it the same and never speak with the mother. Other teachers warn me that the administrator might change the student's final semester grade, but she doesn't. The administrator never refers to the incident again, but the student has a jaundiced view of history for the rest of the semester.

The 1 percent interact with their private schools in a very different way than other New Yorkers interact with their public schools. For example, Ruby, Lily's housekeeper, sends her son, Malcolm, to a public school in Flatbush, Brooklyn. Malcolm is a bright boy, but he is not motivated to work very hard. Ruby doesn't always get advance notice when he is going to get a failing grade on his report card, and he has been asked to attend summer school for several years in a row because he hasn't done well enough during the school year. This news is usually sprung on Ruby, a single parent, at the end of the school year. Malcolm doesn't have any particularly close connections with any of his teachers. Though he is polite, he remains silent in most classes and keeps his head down. Ruby has one ten-minute conference per year with his teachers, but it's held on a day when she has to work (at private schools, parents can come in at hours that work for them, but this type of convenience isn't generally available to public-school parents). She thinks Malcolm will likely get a GED at some point and work with his father, who is a janitor at another public school in Brooklyn.

Ruby is herself getting an associate's degree at Medgar Evers College in Brooklyn, and she would like to work as a paraprofessional, or aide, in an elementary school. She takes one course at a time on Saturday mornings, and, when I arrive at my tutoring session, she sits at the glass dining-room table studying to pass a test on the Civil War for a general history class she is taking. Her older daughter, Cassandra, has done well enough at her public school to earn a scholarship to a City University of New York college, but Ruby isn't quite sure what to do with Malcolm. While studying for her test, she sighs and shrugs. "He'll have to figure it out," she says.

At that moment, Lily's math tutor is leaving the study. I've spent a few minutes chatting with Ruby, which I enjoy, and then I'm heading in to work with Lily. She, like Ruby, is studying the Civil War, and she has to study some primary sources written by Mary Boykin Chesnut, a South Carolinian woman who was married to a Confederate officer and kept a vivid diary during the war. We'll go over every word so that Lily understands the text and its complicated context. Meanwhile, Ruby will be on her own, studying the major battles of the war in the room next door.

The juxtaposed figures of Lily and Ruby toiling in adjoining rooms shows that not all New Yorkers live la dolce vita. They work incredibly hard just to exist in a city where they are cheek by jowl with 8.5 million other souls. Of course, it's far less precarious to be Lily than it is to be Ruby, who lives in her sister's basement off Flatbush Avenue in Brooklyn and did not have health insurance until it was mandated by Obama.

Still, it's not like the rich of New York rest on their laurels. That used to be true. When my husband attended private school in New York City in the 1970s and early 1980s, parents were far less involved in their children's schools. They likely only went to school on back-to-school nights, unless they were actively involved in the parents' association. My husband, who went to Princeton before working in journalism, reports having spent five minutes preparing for the SAT, and that only kids who fared badly the first time around went to an octogenarian tutor for help with the math section of the SAT, which they took for an almost-unheard-of second time. Their major worry was the neighborhood kids who would pelt them with chains and take their money when they were leaving the arcade near school. The tuition for private schools in New York City, which had been emptied by suburbanization in the midst of the city's financial woes, was comparatively less than today, and my husband's private school was filled in part by the kids of professors and struggling actors. When my husband was a senior, his college counselor bellowed at him, "Princeton!" and my husband obeyed. That was, as much as I can tell, the extent of his college-counseling process, partly a testament to his academic chops and partly to the neat pipeline that then existed between his New York City private school and Princeton admissions—a pipeline that is no longer as streamlined as it once was.

Gone are those comparatively halcyon days. The 1 percent work hard, and the 99 percent work hard. Effortless college admissions for the affluent have been replaced by international competition for places at college. Parents don't settle in for boozy lunches but head en masse to Soul Cycle, where they pedal off the pounds. It's not a generation that indulges itself but one that frets over one's place in the world, most strongly symbolized by one's progeny. Kids aren't free to be you and me; they are sculpted into what their parents want of them. My husband rode his bike around New York City as a puny ten-year-old in the 1970s, when the risk of mugging was real; today, kids are hustled from place to place by a phalanx of experts, and they have no time to ride their bikes around Manhattan (and wouldn't be allowed to, anyway). They don't know their own city and don't have the street smarts of earlier generations. Though the city is actually safer now than in the days of the Son of Sam, it still pays to have one's bearings. One boy I taught, who was about five feet five inches and 120 pounds, once ducked through the underpass of the train track on Park Avenue in Harlem to get to his lacrosse practice on time.

He was jumped by two boys who stole his phone in under a minute. Afterward, he admitted, "I guess that wasn't a good shortcut." Many more kids are driven by professional drivers or take Ubers so that they don't have to enter the city's buses or subways.

Their parents worry over them. These are not restful times but times that make everyone feel frenetic. Parents keep in constant touch via text, and kids as young as nine and ten have their own phones. Parents are alerted about their kids' grades and text their kids the minute a low grade is entered into an electronic grade book. The rich don't have time to breathe, unless it's in a hot-yoga class wearing lululemon gear.

Just hearing—not living—the schedules of most of these families makes me tired. After a day of working at a private school and tutoring and putting my son to bed, I'm content just to watch *The Twilight Zone* on Hulu. The families I work with keep going. They delve into their social lives, and benefit parties, and late-night sports practices (hockey teams, for example, have been known to practice at 9:00 or 10:00 p.m. because that's the only time they can get ice time), and sleep is an afterthought, a luxury for the less affluent. The exhaustion of the children of the 1 percent goes unrecognized. I remember one mother, dripping with expensive pearls, telling me, "I just slept over Christmas vacation. I was that bone-tired."

Parents do not turn out the lights and tell their children to go to bed, as they might have during the *Brady Bunch* era. When I wanted to work past ten thirty, my parents told me to get a life and go to sleep. When I was a workaholic, they told me to get some kind of balance in my life. That isn't the lesson these kids get. Their parents allow them to stay up at night, and the kids begin to disintegrate as the week rolls on. Lily in particular gets weepy as Wednesday turns into Thursday, and Friday is a day during which there are a lot of meltdowns at school. Even high schoolers dissolve into tears, and it's often out of sheer exhaustion.

It's easy to tell these kids to be more organized and to practice better sleep hygiene, but the design of their lives makes such advice next to impossible to implement. If a kid plays on a school team that returns them home at seven or eight at night, it's hard for them to start getting their homework done by a reasonable hour because high schoolers routinely have three or four hours of work. The kids also play on travel teams, and the weekends, when they might rest or get a jump on the week's work, are dedicated to tournaments and travel. Their young lives have the same pace as the lives of CEOs, and sleep is a luxury that they cannot afford.

Insomnia is an evil sprite that steals the sleep of those on Fifth Avenue, even the kids. When the mind hasn't had time to rest or process all day, it spins out of control. Researchers have found that the bodies of children in pressure-filled lives suffer from insomnia, stomachaches, and other somatic issues. There are kids in seventh grade who toss and turn all night, though they've gotten up early and had a full day of sports, both at school and on travel teams outside of school. Sometimes, these complaints allow them to go to the nurse for a short nap or to stay home for the day, an acceptable—perhaps the only acceptable—way for them to get off the carousel for a short time.

When I first started working at New York City private schools, I was taken aback by the parents' anger and angst. But now I understand the entire lifetime that has brought them to this point. If their children have learning issues, their paths have been particularly fraught. In the old days, learning issues were not generally diagnosed or understood. Today, kids can be evaluated for learning issues even as young as the first school years, when it's apparent that they are not acquiring a facility with the sound-symbol associations necessary for learning to read.

Today's teachers have a wealth of knowledge about learning issues, as do many of the parents, and they are hungry for more. But it's expensive to get treatment for these issues in NYC. To get educational accommodations, such as extra time on tests, kids have to be evaluated every three or so years by a neuropsychologist or psychologist. The fee is about $5,000, but it can run up to $10,000. Insurance does not tend to cover any of these costs in New York state. This means that parents who can afford these types of evaluations are able to get them, while other parents have to sacrifice and stress to be able to get their kids the accommodations they need in private schools. In other parts of the country, parents can ask their public-school districts for these evaluations and receive them, but in New York City, the Board of Ed has such a long waitlist that this is all but impossible. Like many aspects of city life, being able to enable accommodations for your child is only accessible to the very wealthy.

But that still doesn't mean it's easy to have a child with learning differences in a New York City private school. It means constantly having to make sure your child's teachers, who may not be trained in special ed, understand how your child thinks and what they need. It also means dealing with teachers who think having learning differences means that you can't achieve at the same level as other kids—although these attitudes are rarer than they were 20 years ago. Most private-school teachers, particularly those at the upper-school level, are trained in their discipline—history, math, biology, or another field. They are not trained to understand dyslexia or ADHD or autism spectrum disorders. Private-school parents, therefore, often have to pay to have their child receive help outside of school, and they have to spend a lot of time educating classroom teachers about their kid's needs—unless there is a really good learning specialist in the picture.

As a result, parents of students with learning issues can get pretty irate, particularly by the time their child enters upper school. They can also be motivated to play a lot of games with their child's profile—meaning that they pull it out at the times they deem it's in their child's best interest to do so and keep it conveniently hidden at other times. Sophie's parents sat on her diagnosis of a language-based learning issue until her middle school was putting pressure on them to take her out of the school. They had known about her disorder for years, and they had sought help outside of school—outside of the eye of administrators who, they thought, would surely ask Sophie to find another school if she were still struggling with sound-symbol associations in third grade. They wanted to conceal the extent of their daughter's struggles from her teachers. They had gotten her into that school in kindergarten, and they wanted her to stay put in what they considered the right school. They had already spent $20,000 on a school consultant, and Sophie had been tutored as a five-year-old to take the ERB, or modified intelligence test, that the school used for admission. It wasn't likely, her parents felt, that they could gain admission for her at another school of the same caliber, and it was far safer to keep her at the school.

When Sophie was struggling in sixth grade, producing high-quality homework that was done with her tutor at that time (not me) and failing almost every reading quiz because she didn't understand the material, the school administrators held a number of meetings with her parents. Maria, her mother, later referred to this period as *the troubles*, making it sound as if it were Belfast in the 1970s. Her parents held out as long as they could, mainly making it seem like Sophie's teachers were at fault. (One had given her the wrong version of the abridgment of *The Odyssey*, another had forgotten to give her extra time on a test, and yet another had forgotten to send her the homework assignment when she was absent.) These were handy targets for a while, and Maria became an expert at scanning her daughter's environment for anything slightly out of place, a teacher who missed too many days of school, a teacher who other students didn't like, a teacher who was leaving—situations that could help her create smoke and mirrors around her daughter's academic performance and the real reasons behind it.

When the smoke cleared, however, it was still obvious

that Sophie was struggling and that no matter who administered her test on *To Kill A Mockingbird* or *A Raisin in the Sun*, she had no memory of what she read. At that point, Maria handed over her daughter's evaluation to the school, and it actually bought her some time. The school was happy to receive this information, which helped them understand what was going on for Sophie, and they asked Maria to hire a reading specialist, which she did, and later a learning specialist, who was me. Over time, Sophie improved and became a B+ student, as she learned how to sound out or decode words and how to read for meaning.

Still, the so-called troubles took a toll on Maria and her husband. They are distrustful of their daughter's school. They give generously to the annual fund, thinking that they must keep in the school's good graces, but they also feel that their daughter's teachers are ready to jump on her at any minute, point out her failings, drag her out of the school, and force her into some lesser institution. Each year, the stakes get higher as Sophie moves toward college and her parents have sunk hundreds of thousands of dollars into her tuition. They want her to graduate from her current school, even if it means living on tenterhooks until she does. (These worries are now solely in their imagination, as none of the teachers at Sophie's school believe she shouldn't graduate.) As a result, though they are wealthy and live in a manner that is luxurious by anyone's standards, their Egyptian-cotton sheets, twin Land Rovers, cashmere stoles, and luxury high-rise don't necessarily mean that they sleep easily at night.

While the rich have their stresses, in practical terms it's

hard to understand why the überwealthy are so fretful about their children. A study conducted by Raj Chetty and colleagues at Stanford (where he then taught) found that when kids grow up, their income is highly correlated with that of their parents, and the income of the top 1 percent skyrockets even from the income of those at the 97th percentile. In other words, if your parents were at the 97th percentile of income (or the top 3 percent), you are likely to earn around $60,000 as an adult, but this amount jumps to $80,000 for those raised in the top 1 percent. (This is a national figure, and the 1 percent in New York are much wealthier.) The children of those at the top are more likely to be employed (except those at the very top, who may not need to work, thanks to trust funds), and they are more likely to go to college.

It seems like the top 1 percent have things sewn up, and yet, that is not what one experiences living among them. Instead, these strivers, these sons and daughters of Gatsby, are, like Gatsby himself, interested in piling up more shirts, hosting larger parties, and chasing something bigger, faster, and better than what they already have. For them, as for Gatsby, the beauty of Long Island, with its sandy shores and woodsy bays, is only a place for more anxiety and competition—not for losing themselves in the peacefulness of the seashore.

3

Creating Harmony

Learning is more relational and less purely cognitive than most people think. If kids like you, they are going to do the work, most of the time. I learned that the tutoring relationship is all about creating harmony between the student and me.

When I was growing up in rural Massachusetts, my piano teacher, a Yankee septuagenarian named Mrs. Green (I would never dream of using her first name, as we were on formal terms with each other) who lived in a Spartan saltbox from the 1730s, would play an accompaniment when I had finally mastered a piece. I was fumbling in the dark when it came to the world of music. I had no idea what music meant, and I needed endless weeks to create some rough facsimile of simple pieces played with one hand. But when I had tried my best, without using the metronome, to play a piece, Mrs. Green treated me to an accompaniment that made my notes, played with clumsy, unfeeling hands, into something transcendent. That's what I try to do as a writing tutor. Each kid produces notes that can be spun out into a tune. They don't understand when they are making music with words, as much as I didn't understand the magical, small notes on the bottom of the page that Mrs. Green effortlessly read and played with her nimble, thin hands.

I have a sense of the magic in the students' lives, and when they start making music with their words, I notice. If they can start a kind of riff, I can help them capture it in their own words. While many private-school teachers feel that writing tutoring is cheating, it is, in reality, not that different from the process professional writers use. It is close to impossible for a writer to get outside her head and understand what will captivate other people. It takes a talented editor to discern the skeins of silver amidst the outpourings of dross. Even Harper Lee had an editor who searched beneath all her writing to find the story of Scout told in *To Kill A Mockingbird*. Her editor was like a talented seamstress who found colorful scraps to use at the bottom of the sewing basket.

There are, of course, tutors who write students' papers for them. When I teach high-school history, some of my students hand in papers that are clearly written by graduate students. With interest, I read a sophomore paper about the Vietnam War that links the bombing of Cambodia to the precipitous decline of American masculinity in the midcentury. The tutor who is behind this paper, likely a graduate-school history student, has developed a sophisticated thesis about the fate of American men that is absolutely mangled in the hands of a tenth grader.

When I ask the student to orally put the thesis into their own words, they stammer, "It was, like, the American men, who, like, didn't feel like men. They were the ones who, like, bombed Cambodia." They look at me with a forced grin, as if that will fill in the gaps in their explanation.

When I press them for what they mean about men not feeling like men, they can only point to one factor, the decline of factory jobs. "Men had to prove themselves, so they went to Cambodia and dropped bombs." I admire the surety with which they present this complicated chain of events. When I point out that they haven't explained the genesis of the Vietnam War, only the segment of the war that inflicted damage on Cambodia, they concede the point. "I was going to get to that, but I ran out of time," they say. "My tutor is coming over tonight, so we can work on it," they reassure me.

Often, students' plans for writing or doing any kind of intellectual heavy lifting involve making appointments with their tutors. One even has *Tutor* as a contact on her cell phone, along with *Mom's driver* and other necessary helpers. While I don't work this way, there are many families on Fifth Avenue who have a retinue of tutors coming and going most of the time. A family of four kids I tutor for a few weeks has so many tutors that they have long ago lost track of the schedule. I often arrive when other tutors are still there, and we telegraph sympathetic messages to each other while working with the children in the family. If one child is with another tutor, I am asked to work with another child, whom I know nothing about. It is kind of like working in a massage parlor or being a waiter. This family is interesting because the mother one day admits to me, "I just had four children in eight years. It was a whirl-wind. Maybe that's why the youngest two can't read," she laughs. I ultimately decide not to work with this family, as I can never make inroads with any one kid, and the mother emails me back a pleasant one-line response when I tell her I'm quitting. I wonder if the kids will even notice that I'm not there anymore.

But this type of triage, being shuttled from kid to kid as a kind of McTutor, is not the kind of work I want to do with my students. I want to draw the music, the essence of their work, from them, and this takes time and knowledge of who they are as people and thinkers. I don't force ideas or words on them. Their work has to be authentic to them. The problem is that the kids I work with sometimes need help finding not only words but entire subjects that they can write about. Kids who grow up on Fifth Avenue have little sense of the magic that surrounds them.

During one of my first tutoring sessions with her, Olivia, who wears a backward-facing baseball cap and dresses like Justin Bieber for Halloween, whips open her closet in her trendy SoHo loft. There, in dozens of clear boxes, are sneak-ers. Boxes and boxes of sneakers. This is artwork, not foot-wear. Olivia's parents buy her limited-edition sneakers—the kinds that NBA stars wear off the court. The kinds that cost several hundreds of dollars. Olivia is in the seventh grade.

When she's at school, she's often on her phone. She wants

to see when the latest shoes will come on the market. Her parents help her sell the shoes at just the right time through an app for similar collectors who are called sneakerheads. She loves the adrenaline rush of acquiring a new pair of shoes and the adrenaline rush of selling them. She is an entrepreneur and not afraid of competing with a world of men to buy and sell sneakers.

When Olivia's parents decide to separate, she gets even more sneakers. She has a husky voice—imagine Kathleen Turner as a thirteen-year-old—but her voice climbs and falls a few registers as she shows me her collection.

"These are Air Jordan 1 Spike Lees," she rasps, pointing at a black-and-blue pair of high-top Nikes with a picture of Spike Lee on the side. "My mom got them for me for $300. They're only sold in Brooklyn!"

I do my own online research—the cynic in me doubting the price tag—and find out that not only is Olivia correct, there's a strange backstory to the shoes. They are similar to what Spike Lee wore in *She's Gotta Have It* while having sex. All of which makes me feel very odd and squirmy around this seventh grader. However, she never mentions their history and keeps her shoes squeaky-clean in their boxes.

When Olivia's mom, now living in a different apartment, comes to visit, she brings a pair of shoes. She's in the fashion industry and has connections with shoe companies. So Olivia comes to pair the pain of her mom's visit and departure with the thrill of getting a new pair of shoes.

School is hard for Olivia. She is actually quite brilliant, but not in the way most teachers can appreciate because she is impulsive and has a hard time reading. The administra-

tion at her school tires of her parents' arguments and the
way they spoil their daughter. Her mother arrives at one
parent-teacher conference that I also attend wearing pan-
cake makeup because she is going to be interviewed about
Fashion Week on the local news. During the conference, the
assistant head of the school continually punts the conversational ball to me because she is weary of asking the parents
to do things that they don't follow through on. "So, Blythe,
you will sit down with Olivia and go through her backpack
to organize it," she informs me. I nod, as she lists all the
other responsibilities that will fall to me. The parents are
silent as they shoot daggers at each other. After the conference, the parents leave, and I spend half an hour debriefing
with the administrator about Olivia. This woman adores
the student but hates her mother. "She's on the make," she
says of the woman, and she hatches a spun-out tale of how
the mother is searching for a rich new husband. I wish more
attention were placed on Olivia, because she needs it.

As Olivia's reading problems become more glaring and
the work becomes harder—her class is reading *Huckleberry
Finn* in seventh grade, far too complicated for that age—Olivia becomes more and more anxious, but she's thrilled that
her parents are willing to buy her limitless pairs of sneakers.
She speaks about them in a rush, words spilling out of her
mouth as the sneakers are piled higher and higher in her
closet, their Lucite boxes giving off a cheery glow. I wonder when the boxes will begin to topple over.

At the end of each tutoring session, Olivia's eyes lose
their hooded quality, and her concentration, almost always
bad, snaps into focus as she proudly removes the lids of her

sneaker containers and allows me to caress the leather shoes inside. And, yet, when it comes to writing about sneakers, she can't get a word out. She is restless, tongue-tied, at a complete loss. But then, she starts to talk about how to get a limited-edition shoe, how to store it, how to sell it, and the words come pouring out of her mouth. I transcribe them for her. They are all her words. She can't write because the screen of her iPad terrorizes her. Dyslexic, she can't spell her way through most words. She had training from a reading specialist, but it didn't stick. I've told her parents that she needs to work intensively with a reading specialist (which I am not), but her surfing and skateboarding and drum lessons get in the way. Her erratic, misspelled, mispunctuated work stares back at her from the screen, taunting her. But the kid can talk. And all I do is get her talking and record what she says. We then work on organizing her words and rearranging them, as well as stitching them together with the right transitions. I haven't given her a single word. It's all her magic, but she couldn't see it.

Part of the problem is perspective. Olivia has little idea that most kids don't collect $500 sneakers or fill their trendy, all-white rooms with clear plastic boxes from floor to ceiling. She has no idea that most American kids don't own the shoes that Spike Lee wore in an '80s movie. If she doesn't realize how different she is, she can't write about it. A writer is an outsider, one who can move between worlds without being part of them, but this kid feels no alienation from her world. All I have to do is show her that for a myriad of reasons, including the luck of the draw, she lives a life that produces a unique riff.

Lily is also unaware of the magic of her world. She invites me to watch an international women's squash tournament at a posh Brooklyn Heights sports club. The players are enclosed in a neat glass cube in the carpeted, mahogany-lined club—a cube that reminds me of one of Olivia's shoeboxes. In excited terms, Lily explains the history of this fabled women's tourney—something every squash player in New York anticipates. In this match, a woman from New Zealand is taking on a powerhouse from Egypt. The young Egyptian woman, clad in a spotless white tank top and flared skirt, is cheered on by her mother, who wears a hijab.

The audience sitting right outside the box looks better dressed than that at any other sporting event I've ever been to. Yellow Lacoste sweaters tossed over their shoulders, they clap with well-manicured hands. They don't at all remind me of the people in the Boston Garden of the 1980s, where I grew up watching the Celtics play to the music of a worn-out organ cranking out "Hava Nagila." The squash audience smells like expensive perfume and cologne, and they are respectful, quiet. I'm afraid to make a noise. Even the players are expected to be ladylike on the court. The Egyptian woman wins, and the audience claps politely. Lily's world seems effortlessly orchestrated.

I return home from the match to find laundry in various stages of progress in the corner of my bedroom. I spend the rest of the evening doing the laundry, descaling my coffee machine, and paying bills. During the workweek, I'm too busy even for these mundane tasks. Tutoring every day after school and on Sundays leaves me little time for much else. The world in which people are able to get really excited about squash makes me restless. I mistake moments of privilege for peak experiences, and I believe that my students and their families are coasting on a never-ending magic-carpet ride.

It is only later that I realize that the world of privilege leaves kids as restless as I was on the evening of the international squash tournament. Psychologists believe that kids should not have all their peak experiences at a young age because they will have nothing to look forward to when they're older. The children of elite New Yorkers, however, have had so many privileged experiences that there is little else they can manage to do. Peaking too early teaches kids that they don't need to work to achieve things and makes the kids have a sense of blasé entitlement. The surfeit of privileged experiences also sets the kids up for depression, as they feel that there is nothing left to do.

Writing is a way that Lily can find a conduit for some of this restlessness. Working on an assignment about *Romeo and Juliet*, she thinks about Juliet, whose parents force her to marry Paris at age thirteen. Lily is, when I first meet her, only a year older than Juliet. She wrestles with whether Romeo and Juliet should marry, and whether Juliet knows her own mind. "She's way too young to get married," she thinks at first.

"Do you think she is right to want to leave her parents?" I ask Lily. The idea of being independent has never occurred to her. When her mother, the bank executive with a perennial tan from sailing, enters the room, Lily sits up straighter. "No, that's wrong," she tells me now. "Her parents only want what's best for her."

"But they force her to marry someone she doesn't love, and they don't even ask what she thinks."

"Everyone was like that in Juliet's world," she reminds me. "They're rich." She says it so patly that it's clear she is not open to discussion or debate on this point. She equates being rich with being bossed around as a child, and this truth is so axiomatic to her that there is no debating it.

Lily writes that Juliet should have waited to marry, should have even entered a nunnery if that were her only option to avoid marrying Paris. She seems to want to give Juliet an out, one in which she doesn't throw off her parents' yoke and disobediently marry Romeo, and one in which she also doesn't have to marry Paris. She wants to create a kind of third door, or escape hatch, perhaps like the one she imagines she can find in which she can still please her parents without playing squash at 5:00 a.m.

This type of intellectual seesawing is good for the mind. Some of my students' parents have complained that writing is so hard for their children. One woman even told me about how her son curled up in a fetal position while trying to write. There is no doubt that outsize struggle is not good for anyone, but controlled struggle, this type of recursive self-doubt, is very good for adolescents, particularly those who are restless. It slows them down a little, takes the sheen off their gilded lives. It teaches them to get beneath the surface of things.

The work of Carol Dweck, the author of *Mindset: The New Psychology of Success*, has been in vogue in recent years, particularly among affluent parents. Dweck believes that kids can get into a fixed mindset in which they are not open to taking on challenges and improving because they are afraid of failing. She encourages parents and teachers to foster a "growth mindset" among children so that kids see their capabilities not as static but as ever-improving with effort. She thus recommends praising kids' attempts rather than their results to keep them hungry to try and achieve more, as kids who are only commended for their achievements may become afraid of no longer achieving. Dweck's work has caught on like wildfire among well-to-do parents, who often believe schools are keeping their kids from achieving their full potential. It's all the rage to fulsomely praise kids' efforts, not their results, and to think, as parents and teachers, that we are correctly using Dweck's growth mindset. It's a great leap forward that we now understand the need to encourage our kids to face their challenges and seek change, but like every other parenting and educational fad, according to Dweck herself, this, too, has been misapplied. We're suddenly all too ready to say that we have a growth mindset or to assume that we do, without understanding that having a growth mindset is not something that people can have all the time. As Dweck expressed in an interview in the *Atlantic*, students alternate between being in a fixed and a growth mindset, and seeking out challenges and addressing them is a longer and more arduous and complicated journey than people realize.

Like most educational concepts, this one has been short-circuited. Ambitious teachers and parents want to make an end run around the difficult process of learning. The truth is that it's hard to understand the process by which kids learn, and it can look like nothing is changing when serious, deep changes are going on. It's not a linear process, and it's of course not without setbacks and reversals. And yet, parents want it to look like the unfolding plot of a movie, in which children, after magically sitting down to work with a benevolent tutor, have been transformed into Jane Austen.

It's hard for kids to grow naturally, to allow their minds to follow along the jagged path of real learning and life, when their paths allow no failure, nothing less than an A. Many parents claim that if kids are allowed to receive a B, their college aspirations will suffer. This may have some truth to it. If kids want to get into very selective schools, they are expected to have all A grades. It is particularly difficult to achieve this type of record at a private school, especially if a student is taking more advanced classwork. I don't know how to answer parents when they make this claim—that their child cannot experiment, cannot accept a B or lower if they want to get into a very competitive college. It's a larger educational issue in which colleges must also look beyond a strict GPA, as some do. In the meantime, the pressure on kids to be uniformly excellent exacts a large toll on them. It's impossible to achieve a growth mindset if failure is not an option and if one's learning curve is always supposed to reflect exponential growth.

Because of the pressure to perform, some of what makes good writing and reading and thinking is directly in opposition to the tenor of life on Fifth Avenue. Good writing might just require boredom and frustration. One wonders whether Jane Austen would have been such an incisive writer had she been married or had a career outside the home. She was quite possibly bored to tears, sitting in a drawing room in Bath on a rainy English winter day, her corsets digging into her ribs. She was likely frustrated and annoyed. She wasn't about to board a private plane to the Caribbean, as Lily often does, that's for sure. What Fifth Avenue wants from its children is results, quantifiable results, and that's not the way writing always works.

After Lily has written a draft in her voice with her words about how Juliet should have joined a convent, her mother, Lisa, the banker with a blond bob, gets involved. I have no idea how she has time to read her daughter's papers while structuring megamillion-dollar deals, but she does. She reads the entire paper and calls me about it at 6:00 p.m., as I've just gotten off the subway in Brooklyn. As I walk by the fruit vendors near Prospect Park, poking the grapes to see if they are clean enough to buy, Lisa asks me what I think of Lily's paper. "My daughter doesn't know *anything*," she declares as the fruit vendor shoves some clementines in a plastic bag for me to bring home to my son. "I mean, what does she know about love? For her to write that Juliet shouldn't have married Romeo, it shows her youth, doesn't it?"

I cannot respond because the answer is obvious. "Lily *is* young," I want to say, and she has written this paper as a fourteen-year-old who doesn't understand why Juliet would run away with the mercurial Romeo. They are both fourteen, but while Juliet is impulsive, Lily is simply scared. Lisa might appreciate that Lily wants Juliet to still cling to the safety of home. It's a totally understandable response for a fourteen-year-old, and one that Lily has explained in terms that make sense to her, but Lisa somehow thinks that there is a wrong and right answer for this essay. "Blythe,

I'm surprised that you would let her write this," she scolds me. "Her teacher will tear this to shreds. *To shreds*," she repeats, in case I didn't understand the metaphor the first time around. Lisa experiences Lily's all-girls' school, which seems to be filled with caring, benign teachers, as a veritable den of wolves, much like I imagine Lisa's work environment on Wall Street.

"The paper is written in her voice," I remind Lisa. "That's what the teachers want—to hear her voice."

"Not if it's wrong," Lisa contends. "But I'll work with her on it," she says, in a voice that implies that she has to clean up my mess. As I head home with the clementines nestled in my plastic bag, I feel ashamed somehow, as though I'd done something wrong. I can imagine how Lily must feel. Everything she says and does is monitored, judged, and she must feel as though she's constantly failing.

Lisa decides to spend much of the next few nights ripping her daughter's paper to shreds—as she imagined the teacher might do—and rewriting it. The product is a forty-five-year-old woman's defense of first love. It's badly written, filled with clichés such as *tender flower* to refer to Juliet and *burning passion* to refer to her love affair with Romeo, and it's clear that Lily's voice has been completely suffocated. No one under forty would refer to Juliet's tryst with Romeo as *deflowering*, making it patently obvious that the fingers of an elder have been all over Lily's paper. As it turns out, her English teacher also tears Lily's paper apart—though gently—and Lily works with me on rewriting the paper and submitting it while her mother is on a business trip to France. While writing the final draft, Lily is merely weary. She accepts that Juliet needs to rebel and leave her family. This is what will happen to Lily in the end, I think. Her mother will tire her into leaving home and separating from her parents, even though Lily doesn't really want to and her mother plans to keep her daughter enmeshed for her whole life.

Trevor is peeved about having to work over summer vacation. Though he wants to work with his building's janitor over the summer, power-washing gum because he loves working with his hands and seeing the immediate results, he's working for the month of July at the major Wall Street bank where his dad is high up in the chain of command—so high that when Trevor arranges to meet me at his father's office to work on summer reading and writing, we are treated so obsequiously that I feel on edge. A squad of assistants meets us in the waiting room. The father is busy in a meeting, but as we walk down the silent corridor, the red carpet on the floor makes me think of Charlton Heston as Moses in *The Ten Commandments*. It's as if the Technicolor Red Sea is parting before me and Trevor, with hapless Egyptian charioteers being tossed aside. As the scion of the boss, Trevor has that power. I half expect an assistant to hand us carved stone tablets, but she just hands us some Perriers instead, nested on thick napkins with the firm's logo emblazoned on them.

The squad of assistants ushers us into a conference room with a table that would fit the entire Israeli–Palestinian negotiating team with a lot of room left over. Trevor flips open the minibar in a way that suggests this place is his home and removes a Toblerone candy bar that he begins to devour. The squad of assistants reminds me of the minions from *Despicable Me*. They are all wearing the same type of clothing and move en masse to make sure that Trevor and I are well situated along the gleaming oak conference table. It's hard to calm down from the fuss and make Trevor do some writing on the novel *Passing* by Nella Larsen. He seems distracted and fidgets with the cocktail napkins. It's not easy being Moses's son.

The book that Trevor has to write about is amazing, but it's a world away from the hushed walls of the bank in many ways. Published in 1929, *Passing* is about a light-skinned Black woman who reunites with a long-lost childhood friend, another light-skinned woman who passes as white and is married to a racist white man. The book was written during a time when passing was fraught with danger, as the plot makes clear. But still today, people can pass in many ways, and they can present themselves as something they're not, in inauthentic ways, to the world.

Trevor's assignment is to write about an instance of passing in the present day. It's a deceptively simple assignment that can be interpreted in many ways. It can be interpreted literally, as, for example, a person from a group who passes him or herself off as a member of another group—such as an LGBTQ+ person who pretends to be straight. But the assignment can also be interpreted more metaphorically and psychologically, and this is where I wonder if Trevor will go. He is, in my mind, very different from the way he is being marketed to the world. Sitting with his Brooks Brothers jacket, repp tie, and leather shoes, he looks every inch the junior banker. But underneath, he dreams of surfing, of cruising down the Pacific Coast Highway in a vintage VW bus. He is also someone who is altogether too fond of slipping a vape pen into his pocket at the corner store without paying for it.

I give him several prompts to think about other instances of passing, and what he comes up with surprises me.

"I know a lot of girls who have passed, I mean in the way they try to show off to me," he says. At first, I think he's being boastful, until the flush on his face reveals that he is embarrassed by what he is about to say. "I mean, they act all interested in me, and one of them even pretended she was pregnant."

I don't have a poker face, so I imagine I look like my eyes are bugging out as I ask him to explain. Keep in mind he's sixteen years old.

"Well, she said she was pregnant," he tells me. "She was late a few days."

"Do you use birth control? I know that your school nurse has condoms." This is what the health educator at my school would want me to say, and I say it because I don't know what else to say.

"Of course I do. She said it slipped. But it was just a lie. She just said that because she likes attention. And I didn't force her."

In graduate school, I was often told that I intellectualize when I should be emoting. This is one of those times that the defense mechanism comes in handy. "How do you see this as passing?" I ask him, eager to return to books over his personal problems.

"Just teenagers. They act like they are so serious, but they don't really care about each other. She is now dating my friend. And she wasn't pregnant."

"So you think pretending to feel a certain way but faking it is passing?" I ask him.

"Yeah, that's it. Faking it. Everyone does it."

Trevor realizes he can't use this story exactly, though it would make a very good story in many ways, but he writes a story about a girl who pretends to be really interested in a boy whom she then dumps when his friend shows interest in her. I don't ask many more questions about the source material on which this story is based—the girl he was involved with. His version of the story is that the boy was left feeling abandoned at the end, and that people pass as interested in love when they're not. I ask him to think about how the girl feels in the story, but he can't get much beyond her need for constant attention. I think, looking around the room, he's far too young for all of this—the situation with the girl, the bank, the repp tie.

Though his paper is filled with run-ons, misspellings, and misplaced modifiers, the dialogue is good. He remembers everything that girls have said to him, and it shows up in this story. At one point, the girl takes several selfies in his bedroom and posts them on Snapchat or Instagram or whatever the social networking site of the moment is, and her friend, who also likes him, gets pissed and flames her. The b-word is rapidly exchanged, though Trevor removes some of this from his paper. All of the characters seem deserving of pity and pathos in the end.

That story has all the savor of bittersweet chocolate to me. It's rich and bitter and hard to digest. It's difficult to

cry over a boy whose father has a herd of assistants in a
bank—or is it? When I leave this type of tutoring situation,
I long for the regularity of the subway ride back to Brooklyn or Queens, even with its jolts, stuffed compartments,
and delays on the Manhattan Bridge. This is more real and
understandable to me—the train touching the steel tracks,
and the angst of people trying to get home. All that makes
sense to me, while little of Trevor's life does.

The book *Passing* has resonated with Trevor. Though
he clearly leads a troubled personal life and I worry that he
is not aware of how to treat young women, the book he
is reading has meant something to him. However, more
often, the students I work with misinterpret their reading,
and it is my job to make it resonate with them, to create a
kind of translation through which they can understand it.

It's interesting that students always say that there is no
right and wrong answer when it comes to reading because
there actually are some very wrong answers and interpre-
tations at times. In fact, students can badly miscalculate as
readers. But it's not entirely their fault, as they are often
asked to read books that are way over their heads. Private
schools pride themselves on offering demanding curricula,
but no matter how precocious or verbal some of their students are, a text may be too mature or psychologically complicated for them. As I work one-on-one with students, I
can see these miscalculations.

Sophie chooses not to read Frederick Douglass's powerful
autobiography of his experiences of, and escape from, slavery. Instead, she decides to read some kind of CliffsNotes-
type summary online. The problem is that she has deprived

herself of the power of the words, and she has unwittingly chosen a site whose unnamed author has also apparently not read Frederick Douglass's autobiography. That's why Sophie produces a breezy paper that speaks about how Frederick Douglass went hunting with his master and how Douglass was not just ambivalent (which he was not) but downright pained to escape northward from the plantation.

After reading her draft, I'm speechless for several minutes. "Did you read the book?" I ask her.

"Parts of it," she says, chewing the glitter paint off her nails and texting her friends.

"I don't think enslaved people were allowed to have guns," I tell her. "Can you find me the part of the text where Douglass goes hunting with his slave master?"

She flips randomly through the unmarked pages of her book until she admits, "Well, for part of it, I used a website." She finds the site online, and the background is marked with stars and rainbows. It's clearly pitched at very young children, and the author is badly misinformed. "See," she says. "It says here that Frederick Douglass loved his master and went hunting with him."

"Sophie, does that sound right?" I ask her. "What was the nature of slavery?"

She has so badly misunderstood this book and Douglass's entire point—that the slave system kept him in psychological and physical fetters—that I don't know where to begin. Instead, I ask Sophie to read aloud. The words are beautiful but incisive, describing the pain of Douglass's not having known his mother, of seeing his aunt whipped by a jealous slave master, of his own degradation and enlightenment as he learns to read from a friendly slave mistress who is then chastised by her husband never to teach an enslaved person to read. Sophie doesn't say anything, and her eyes stay on the book. When she opens the Google Doc with her paper, she drags her cursor over everything she has written thus far and deletes it. I hope reading has done the same thing to her misconceptions about slavery—forced her to start totally anew.

Lily is a more perceptive reader than Sophie. She can relate to feeling out of place and misaligned with her reality. She is, at fifteen, moonfaced, still pudgy, and she describes her all-girls' school as *female hell*. Her school makes her wade through literature that's impossible even for many adults, such as *Paradise Lost* by Milton. She has attentional issues that make this wading difficult, but she listens very carefully when we read out loud. She likens the devils in Milton's epic, who are expelled from heaven and sent to the deepest reaches of hell, to girls at school. "It's like the social scene at my school," she ventures. We laugh about the labors of the teenagers vying for the most popular girl's favor, in the same way that the fallen angels want to get back into God's grace. The devils are jealous of Adam and Eve just like the mean girls at Lily's school are jealous of the new popular girl, the one who moved in from New Jersey and has become the new queen bee. Milton's cosmos, so confusing to me, makes complete sense to Lily after it's been mapped onto the world of competitive sophomore girls. These are Beelzebubs in Burberry.

She is a gifted reader because she feels the literature so deeply. She notices things that I don't because she reads so slowly and carefully, and she thinks for a minute after she reads that Satan's new tactic is to use guile to enter God's domain. "Guile," she muses, "in the world before social networking. What would that even mean? Now, Hell is an Instagram post...or worse, a Snapchat image." She has been left out of parties while other girls post selfies of themselves at parties on Facebook or Instagram or send her Snapchat photos. For her, Satan's lair is filled with photos of the parties she was left out of (it's ironic, because in Milton, the devils were left out of the ultimate party), so she understands hell on a very intimate level. For Lily, the Garden of Eden is likely a place where there is no squash practice, no devilishly mean girls, no SATs.

Reading, when done right, can also cause disequilibrium among Gatsby's children. A boy in a class on personal finance I teach at a private school is so disquieted by the simple observation that one's view of finance is affected by one's social class that he becomes irate. "This is just more liberal propaganda," William spews, using his fingers to comb back his thick black pompadour. "I'm sick of teachers trying to cram this stuff down my throat."

I'm so taken aback simply because I haven't foreseen any minefields in the material. The students are enrolled in a short course that asks them to practice skills related to making a budget, investing, and saving. The text we are reading seems so axiomatic to me that I have not anticipated this controversy. The author makes the point, perhaps too sophisticated for high-school students, that if one is brought up with money, one may not always think about it or its consequences. If one isn't brought up with money, it may be more of an issue. Is that provocative? William, whose parents work on Wall Street, thinks so.

"I just don't buy this crap," he says, taking over the conversation and not letting the point go.

"So you don't think that one's class affects the way one views money?" I ask him. The irony, sitting heavily in the room, is that he is proving, with his angry words and flushed face, that one's privileged status makes one at times oblivious to the fact that people from other classes see money in different ways. There are other students in the room, some students of color, some students on scholarship (not necessarily the same kids), so I ask the rest of the class if anyone has a different point of view. I can't make a difference here. William will discount anything I say, so I hope one of the students will contribute a different point of view. However, most are long wearied by trying to fight William and his confident pronouncements, and they are all silent, save a blond girl clad in lululemon yoga pants who backs up everything he says. Still, the words from the reading hang there, and William's anger attests to how much what he has read has knocked him off guard.

A few days earlier, he seems to be enjoying himself as we get a special tour of the Stock Exchange, rare in the post-9/11 world, and we watch from the balcony above as a company has a moderately unsuccessful IPO. There are even players from the NFL on the floor of the exchange, and we mingle with them freely. In my mind, the other teacher and I have provided a once-in-a-lifetime experience for these students, but after the short class is over, William and his friend give us very low ratings as teachers and cite our lack of knowledge as the reason. They were hoping, they write, for a class on economics, a kind of mini–MBA, not a class that lectured them about their social class. They would have liked to read and talk about money in the abstract, separate from socioeconomic status, if such a thing is possible.

This is why *The Great Gatsby* resonates with Park Avenue so thoroughly, even today, and seems so ironic when taught to students like William. All the characters, save Myrtle and George, are wealthy. (Nick, the narrator, is not wealthy but has access to the rich.) The hero, Gatsby, is fantastically wealthy, but he comes from a different class from the Buchanans. Daisy and Tom do not represent the class that most of today's wealthy children come from. Gatsby's children do not generally come from old money; they come instead from strivers, from people who have, like Gatsby, built mansions so they can look at the green light across the bay that stands for Daisy and old money. *The Great Gatsby* is in many ways an indictment of the heedless pursuit of wealth, but Gatsby's charm and the romantic shading that Fitzgerald gives him make him endearing to the students. It is the one book I've noticed that the children of the 1 percent truly love universally.

The one student I tutor who does not like *The Great Gatsby* is Carmen, a student who attends an Upper East Side girls' school through an access program that helps students of color prepare for and attend private day and boarding schools. Her program has asked me to work with her on a pro bono basis because she is not handing in her work and is struggling with writing. Carmen lives in Fitzgerald's valley of ashes, in Corona, Queens, in what Nick Carraway considered the no-man's-land between Long Island and Man-hattan. The book does not speak to her.

Carmen is, in fact, turned off by most of her schoolwork. Her parents, who are immigrants from Colombia, want her to do well, and they are worried about her. Though she is clearly bright, she has given up on herself. She doesn't take notes in class, she doesn't read the books she's assigned, and she doesn't want anyone to know how badly she's doing. We meet in the cafeteria at her school, and when her English teacher asks to meet with me, I ask Carmen why. "She meets with all the students' tutors," she tells me, though the teacher later tells me this isn't true and that she is worried about Carmen. Most of her school curriculum doesn't speak to Carmen, either.

Other books don't hold most students' attention. *Beloved* by Toni Morrison features a confusing, winding narrative about rape, slavery, and infanticide. It is so difficult that many students even miss the central scene, in which Sethe kills her own child rather than have her return to slavery. "Did the baby die?" one student asked me. "I missed that entirely." It is easy to miss, buried in the dense, swirling text. Some white students dread learning anything about civil rights. Not all, by any measure, but it always surprises me that they sigh when they are about to embark on a study of civil rights or read a book like Frederick Douglass's autobiography.

When I teach American history at a private school, I am thrilled to be able to show the students *Eyes on the Prize*, the lauded documentary about the civil rights movement. We have been through so many topics that did not speak to them—everything from the War of 1812 to tariffs to the silver standard controversy (which, in actuality, some strangely cottoned to)—that I think, *Finally, a topic they can get excited about.*

Eyes on the Prize is compelling watching. An eerily calm narrator explains each step of the civil rights movement, starting with the brutal murder of fourteen-year-old Emmett Till, an African American boy visiting relatives in small-town Mississippi, who was killed by local whites. His mother made the brave decision to have an open casket to show the world her son's battered body (which had been weighted and sunk in the river). It could not be described as *boring. Disturbing*, yes. *Unsettling*, yes. *Uncomfortable*, absolutely.

Many of my sophomore history students, all white except for one half-Asian student, are rude as we watch the footage of hoses being turned on student protestors, some as young as middle-school students or younger, in the streets of Birmingham in 1963. "We already watched this in seventh grade," complains one student who is usually stellar. I have to subject them to a quiz on the movie to make them watch. Instead of being riveted by the footage, they watch under duress, with the fear of punishment. To me, there is nothing as compelling as watching footage from that era, of people who just won't take abuse anymore, but it really upsets these students. Later, I feel that I have erred in punishing the kids rather than speaking to them openly about why they are so resistant. I have taken away the attention from their resistance to learning about civil rights and made it about some superficial classroom disturbance, which al-

lows all of us to skirt the discomfort beneath issues of race.
I hope their discomfort stays with them and chafes at them
until they are ready to examine and consider it.

Every once in a while, there's a kid who surprises me,
who produces from God knows where a real sense of compassion in reading and writing. There is one who looks
like Elvis in one of my history classes who really gets Rosa
Parks's humility. He watches additional hours of footage of
the Montgomery Bus Boycott and does a spot-on imitation of Parks: "I just did what anyone would do," he says
in a quiet, level voice. "It was no big deal." He completely
understands her vibe, her approach. He is wealthy, just like
many of the other kids, but he knows how to read people
and understands how much Parks's humble words belied her
intent and the momentousness of her decision.

For the kids on Fifth Avenue, their best moments can
come from little things like understanding the understate-
ment of Rosa Parks. Everything else in their worlds is big,
writ very large. They can return from the weekend—a
weekend when I am happy simply to have bought French
cookies at an upscale grocery store called Fairway—and
report that they had been introduced to Bono at a concert
and had gone skiing. Or they went to the Hamptons and
had gone shopping for clothes at the newly opened Ralph
Lauren boutique (they were surprised I hadn't heard about
it) and had worked out with their mother's personal trainer.
Vacations are even more extreme. The two weeks off for
spring break are a time when I see my husband and son,
make sure the fridge is better stocked than usual, maybe
make chocolate chip cookies, watch more old movies on

Netflix, and—if I am lucky—see a movie in the theater. Not so my students.

The second school lets out, Lily is whisked by her parents to exotic locales. Morocco one year, the ski resort at Alta quite often, and once on an ecotour of Cambodia. She Segways across cities, she goes to the markets, she stays in five-star hotels. On New Year's Eve, she is on a yacht watching fireworks in St. Barths. She runs into people she knows while drinking in the Caribbean. She has a tan. Before she leaves for the French Riviera, she has been bought an entirely new wardrobe, complete with new Lilly Pulitzer dresses and cover-ups, sunglasses, and sandals. The idea of buying a wardrobe for one trip is foreign to me, quite literally. She returns the minute before school starts again and spends most of the week exhausted from jet lag.

Trevor, the closest thing to a modern-day Buchanan, goes to some island where you have to be an ancestral member of the family to live there. When he first tells me about it, I think it is some kind of joke.

"No, really," he explains. "It's owned by my family—and other relatives."

He seems content to spend a lot of time there on spring and fall weekends and during the summer. I gather that there is a lot of unsupervised time, during which he and his cousins drink in a family boathouse and play in the water.

Trevor is particularly close to his cousin Julia, who is his age and whom I've also tutored. He tells me that Julia has already been to drug rehab at age sixteen and that she is trying to stay away from drinking. "She's always posting pictures of herself next to drugs," he tells me. "But she's just a liar." He shows me photos from his phone of himself with Julia, a girl with long straight frosted hair who is wearing a low-cut T-shirt, cutoff jeans. They spend most of their summer weekends on their ancestral island. "There are no Jews there," he informs me, laughing, and I'm not sure if he is apologizing or making sure I know that I would not be invited.

"Really?" I ask him. "Are you sure? Some might have sneaked in without your knowing."

He nods. I've noticed before that he is nervous about the fact that I'm Jewish, and he wants to clearly delineate the space that his family goes to. I wonder if there are any people of color on his island and if restrictions are something he has heard about at home.

In spite of their glamour, these experiences create little impression on children who are used to a constant stream of delights. They pass by students in a kaleidoscope of colors and textures, and they are surely beautiful, but they do not cause the harmony that results in good writing or thinking. The truth is that leading a boring, uneventful life is good for kids. It gives them something to look forward to. Researchers have found that overindulgence, including providing too much entertainment and loose discipline, results in kids who lack proper boundaries and who need constant and immediate gratification. Experts believe that if kids have too many peak experiences early in life, they will have nothing to look forward to. If you've already met Bono and know the head of Nike and have Segwayed across Laos, what more is there for you to do? Life acquires a kind of flat quality. The result is depression, feeling that nothing else lies ahead of you. There is no hunger in your belly for anything, and you feel listless, ill at ease.

4

Hothouse Flowers

I learn that sometimes, the kids simply aren't all right. The longer I tutor, the more the specter of Freud appears in the hallways, the cocktail lounges, the coffee bars of the Upper East Side.

As finals approach during her sophomore year of high school, Lily's room becomes a hive of round-the-clock tutoring. Her chemistry tutor is in such great demand on the Upper East Side that he has to come at eleven at night because that's the only slot he has open. She texts her mother repeatedly to make sure that the tutor has been lined up because she feels certain she will fail without his help. She is already exhausted and will now stay up until at least midnight to work with this sage.

"Isn't there anyone else who could help you in chemistry?" I ask her innocently, knowing my skills do not extend to that subject.

"My class is taught by a PhD chemist from Columbia," she sobs, tears dripping down her face. "Only this tutor can help me! He works with everyone at my school." Based on her stories, it seems like her teacher has no experience teaching kids. He says extra-help sessions are "spoon-feeding" and complains bitterly that kids expect him to chew their food up before they swallow it. He also follows a model called *student-directed learning*, which seems to involve kids teaching themselves. Though he thinks no one in his class should get extra help, the irony is that all his students are being helped by a brilliant Princeton grad who pays his rent in Crown Heights just from tutoring students at Lily's school. I vaguely know this tutor, as he calls me occasionally to get business from the other kids at my school. I never refer kids to him, as he has no experience or training working with students with learning differences. He seems acceptable with other kinds of kids, but he is mainly focused on his fledgling music career.

With nearly endless resources at their disposal, kids like Lily spend years getting tutored. Some even start working with college advisers in middle school, and others start getting tutored for the SAT or ACT in ninth grade. When the tutoring picks up in eleventh grade, the kids have to take full-length SAT or ACT practice tests each weekend. That means hours and hours of test-taking. They practice endless questions, and some do well as a result of this never-ending drilling.

The result of all this meddling in their children's lives—and we haven't even touched on college admissions yet, a whole war in itself—is that many kids achieve beyond their ability, so that tutoring has to follow them to college. Others like Lily contend with horrible anxiety.

Lily and Sophie are above average academically, but they attend schools at which their English teachers write well-received novels and their French teachers screen absurdist movies in French without subtitles. I often wonder how they wound up in schools that they have no business attending. The answer is that their parents began thinking about applying for their children to attend schools shortly after their children's births. There is a Manhattan consultant who charges over $20,000 to place kids in kindergarten, one of an army of consultants who are crisp, well educated, and professional. They use terms such as *school fit* and *match* and *development*. They have an entire jargon about a process that is essentially about money and prestige.

When kids are young, like four, it's not really clear how academically strong most of them will be. What is clear is what their parents do, where they live, and how much they make. That's why it benefits the rich to get their kids placed in kindergarten, or even before if the schools start earlier (attending the right nursery school is also necessary in parts of New York). I discover from speaking to the admissions staff at the school where I work that there are feeder schools for kindergarten. To get a leg up, you first have to start your kid at Park Avenue Christian Church Day School (which later moved to the West Side, dropping the *Avenue,* among other words) or some similarly pricey and exclusive school.

Kids are interviewed for kindergarten. When I work at a tony Manhattan private school, prekindergartners in formal clothing show up with their extremely well-dressed parents to interview for kindergarten spots. It seems like a lot of pressure for a preschooler. I see parents yelling at their kids outside the school—I am never sure if that is pre- or postinterview. The parents, in their power suits or designer dresses and heels, look steely and determined.

I tutor kids when they're older, so I'm not sure how some of them got into the elite, demanding schools they attend. From seeing their photos at earlier ages, I gather that they were very cute, and their parents must have done most of the talking at the school interviews. They are full-pay students, whom schools covet. Many students are tutored for the ERBs, the modified intelligence tests that kids must take to get into the early grades in New York City private schools. These tests are not supposed to be teachable, but some enterprising private-school moms, worried about their own kids' chances of getting into private school, realized that the tests are modified IQ tests and that kids could be tutored in them. This was a brilliant business idea but makes it difficult for the schools to judge which kids can really handle their curriculum because wealthy kids are routinely prepped for the tests.

It is only after years of tutoring Sophie, who has language-based learning differences, that her mother, Maria, admits that she had Sophie tutored for the ERBs when she was in kindergarten. "She did really well!" she remarks, and it has been shown that kids can receive a temporary bump in IQ scores through tutoring. However, the results are only temporary, and then kids revert. This is what happened to Sophie, as her mother, shaking her head, admits, "But it didn't last." As a four-year-old, Sophie was pumped full of vocabulary words and information, and she quickly lost the meaningless clutter that had been deposited into her young head.

Many people collude in making it possible for kids who struggle to gain admission to—and remain at—private schools that are too difficult for them. As Sophie's tutor, I'm part of this situation, though I'm trying to improve her skills and help her to be a better writer and thinker. When I speak with Sophie's teacher after her mom suggests I "liaise with the teacher," the teacher uses a kind of coded language that veils how truly difficult English class is for Sophie.

"I'm glad she's getting outside support," her teacher tells me. *Support* can be used euphemistically in a way that clouds how much work students need to do outside of class to keep up. Though I never write students' papers, some tutors do— or at least their editorial fingerprints are all over their tutees' work. Many teachers deplore this situation, but others are fine with it, because it means the students can keep up in a class in which they are overmatched.

"Sophie really needs to dig into the text and unpack what she reads," the teacher continues, using two clichés that are common among many private-school English teachers. The metaphorical images are helpful to me, but to Sophie they are meaningless. She can't even understand the language of the quotes she reads in books such as *The Great Gatsby*, much less dig into and unpack them. Private-school teachers like to couch their comments in this type of language to obscure the fact that some of the students don't really have the skills to grapple with the material. "Sophie wrote an unmoored essay," the teacher goes on to say. "She really needs to tether it to the text." The woman's metaphors make me want to drool, they are so beautiful. I just love the idea of tethering an essay to the text, but the woman might as well tell Sophie she needs to figure out how to create a thermonuclear shield for incoming ballistic missiles. The task means nothing to Sophie in those terms, and the English teacher avoids the plain fact that Sophie's skills are just not yet good enough to tackle the assignments in her class. Instead, it is left to me to help Sophie find excerpts from the text to back up the points she is trying to make in her essay.

Much of the work that kids are supposed to be doing occurs between adults. There are rounds of meetings and calls between me and Sophie's teacher and between her parents and her teacher. Sophie spends very little time meeting with her teacher directly because she says the teacher stresses her out, so the adults talk endlessly among themselves. There is a great deal of fretting, negotiating, and note-taking on her parents' part during these meetings, but Sophie does very little of the work herself. Instead, she waits for her sessions with me or her other tutors to get her assignments done, meaning that she's always several removes from her own work. Though the writing she submits is always her own, I break down each part of the process for her, asking her, for example, to go into the text to find quotes and then to underline key words in each quote and explain them. She does this willingly with me, but she refuses to work much in class or directly with her teacher. Her parents claim she feels "stigmatized" by the other kids when she asks questions in class, so Sophie remains mum in the back row. Somehow, her academic work has become all too similar to the way she orders pizzas to arrive at her Manhattan school for lunch. The Uber Eats deliveryman brings the pies to the front desk, and she meets him there and totes the food to a classroom to devour with her friends. She doesn't eat in the school cafeteria—even though there's perfectly well-prepared food that's included in the tuition—but instead she orders in. She doesn't work directly with her teacher but waits until her tutors, similar to her pizza delivery man, can bring the goods directly to her. As a result, her parents are paying about half of the cost of the tuition again in tutoring fees, and Sophie is missing out on working with her English teacher, who is the best person to guide her in her own course.

To their parents' delight, a handful of little kids are very verbal and precocious. They grow up to be excellent students, and a competitive private school is okay for them in some ways. Other kids like Lily and Sophie are just rich, and their parents are aggressive and have every base covered. New York City private-school parents usually are of a certain type that passes muster with the admissions staff. They are well-dressed and present themselves well. They are consummate game players. They can be aggressive when needed, but they are also able to flatter and wheedle their way into getting what they want. They seem agreeable on the surface—some of them—but they can really dig in when snowplowing, or clearing their children's path of obstacles, is required. They can use the euphemisms of education, including terms such as *needing support,* or intensive tutoring, for their kids who don't quite make the grade, and they know what's required of them. They show up for meetings, back-to-school nights, fundraisers, and committees. They dress Christmas trees, fasten lights to Hanukkah menorahs and Kwanzaa kinaras, appear at Parent Association meetings in designer dresses, and send administrators and college counselors silk scarves and ties.

I'll never forget my first holiday season at a private school, when parents, mostly moms, show up on a snowy day dressed in Canada Goose coats and fur-lined boots to decorate a mammoth live evergreen with school-related ornaments, including teddy bears dressed in school sweaters. The tree, along with the Kwanzaa and Hanukkah candleholders, looks stunning. Many of the mothers formerly worked in banking or corporate law, and they are perfectionists who now devote themselves to making the school lobby look like a Hollywood set. Every time I pass the tree, I feel a kind of electric shock of joy, like I did when I visited my Christian friends' houses growing up. Though I'm the kind of Jew who occasionally has a Christmas tree, my squat little trees aren't decorated like this one. Passing that tree makes me feel like I can glimpse, for a few seconds at a time, what it's like to have a holiday that involves a month-long dive into everything that's beautiful and restorative, including evergreens, glitter, bows, and wrapped packages. The mothers who decorate the tree seem to have the Midas touch, turning the linoleum floors and tile walls to gold. It takes me a while to see that all that glitters isn't gold.

Guided by parents who are polished, poised, and steel-

nerved, some kids wind up at schools where they are totally *overmatched*, to use the educational consultants' jargon,
and this becomes very apparent by middle and high school.
Some private schools allegedly make a practice of accepting rich kids who they know won't make it to senior year,
and, after soaking their families for the tuition and donations in the early years and giving the children very cute
uniforms that give the parents bragging rights (everyone
knows which outfits belong to which schools), they wash
these kids out and force them to go to other, supposedly
lesser schools. However, every once in a while, I meet a
kid who has somehow survived against all odds. It is usually because this kid has a phalanx of experts. People with
PhDs help them write history papers in eighth grade. Columbia grad students help them write English papers. What
no one does is actually make sure the kids can read. That
is my domain as a learning specialist.

Sophie is an expert at mastering whatever her teachers or
tutors put in front of her, even if she doesn't really understand it. Like her parents, she is a consummate game player.
It is actually staggering that this child has faced a curriculum in which she had to write about *The Odyssey* in sixth
grade and analyze the French Revolution in eighth grade,
but clearly she was buoyed by an army of experts. She par-
rots back what her teachers have said about the Lorraine
Hansberry play *A Raisin in the Sun* but doesn't have a clue
what it means to live in a segregated community (though
she largely does live in one). "I mean, Beneatha, like, has
the dream, like, that she wants to live in a segregated com-

munity," she tells me, speaking about one of the main characters in Hansberry's play.

"Do you mean *integrated*?" I ask her. "Beneatha wants to
live in an *integrated* community and move away from a *segregated* community."

"Yes, *integrated*. I always get that confused with *segregated*,"
she admits, looking at the texts on her phone.

Anyone who lived through segregation could not forget
that word, but these concepts are entirely abstract to Sophie. She does her writing and reading at several removes
from the material, believing that she cannot do anything
without consulting a flotilla of adults, which removes her
sense of agency.

Trevor, also a lackluster student, is put through the paces
on the athletic field. He has been playing soccer on a competitive travel team since middle school. Even in seventh
grade, he had practices until 10:00 p.m., didn't get home
until close to eleven, and didn't get into bed until nearly
midnight. He is away on most weekends. His father, with his
graying hair and sober face, looks like someone at Meghan
Markle's wedding (from Harry's side of the family), and
anxiously peers onto the soccer field while speaking on his
phone and pacing back and forth on the sidelines. He can
really dress Trevor down after a disappointing game. Once,
after Trevor asks me to attend a game and I want to show
him support, I sit in front of his dad on the sidelines, but my
nerves become so jangled from his screaming at the coaches
and referees and Trevor that I move to another seat. Before
one tutoring session, I have to wait in Trevor's room while

I hear his father bellow at him, calling him an "embarrassment, not worthy of being on the team!" because he feels his son played badly in the game that afternoon. His father would have done well as a parent in ancient Sparta. Some kids like Trevor spend so much time playing their sport that they literally wear out their body. One student I taught irreparably injured his shoulder playing tennis before he could even get to college, thereby ending his dreams of attending college to play tennis.

His Lordship is generally cordial to me, though I see him quite rarely. He pours me club sodas from glass bottles in his bar and is careful to include a cocktail napkin so the drink won't bleed onto the mahogany desk. Occasionally, I feel what it's like to be Trevor when his father directs withering criticism my way.

Once, after I've entered the apartment and his father takes my coat, he surprises me by actually speaking with me. Sticking my broken-spined cheap black umbrella in the Chinese porcelain stand that contains Burberry umbrellas, he asks, "Does Trevor use the extra time he has at school?" Trevor has been granted extra-time accommodations on tests at his school because he has a diagnosed learning issue and ADHD, but his father has adamantly opposed his son's use of any accommodations, which he considers cheating. He has remarked in the past, snickering, "What's Trevor going to do, have extra time in life?" By carrying this argument to its extreme (just because Trevor uses extra time on taking tests, it doesn't mean he will need it on other tasks), his father has made the whole debate ridiculous. When he asks me if Trevor uses his accommodations at school,

I have to admit that I don't know, and he barks, "Well, if you don't know, then who does? I'm not home enough to collect more than core samples on my son. I rely on you to keep track of these things!" Unpacking this quote, as Sophie's English teacher would ask her to do, I am fixated on the words *core samples*. I'm not sure if that phrase is tossed around in the world of management consulting, but the words have a kind of clinical, scientific feel to them. I keep imagining petri dishes with droppers. His wife, generally silent and regal and very tall, appears, arms folded across her chest. She wears a sour expression on her face, but I can't tell whether it's for her husband or for me. Either way, the conversation is at an end.

I fret all during the tutoring session that follows, and my obsessive side keeps asking me *Why didn't I know whether Trevor uses extra time?* until, finally pulling into my home stop on the subway, I recover enough psychological awareness to realize this is the way Trevor must feel all the time—lesser than, failing, guarded. I nurse an ambivalence toward Trevor's father and often conduct internal arguments with him as I'm walking up Fifth Avenue to the imposing facade of their apartment building, which I imagine is scowling down at me. *You're the father*, I say to him in my imagination. *How am I supposed to know these things if you don't?* In more flippant moods, I ask him, *Deflect much?* But this is all in my head. In person, I am reserved but polite. I'm careful not to engage him in too much chitchat and just want to get to the tutoring session with his son.

Keep in mind that kids like Trevor don't need athletic scholarships. They can afford college hundreds of times over. In fact, they are more likely to get into college by their parents writing an additional check to the development office than by their athletic skills, but they play on. When kids want to play Division I sports, particularly in the Ivy League, they have to meet the standards laid out in NCAA-designed indexes that include their grades and SAT scores. Colleges usually don't accept kids from elite private schools to play sports unless they are at the very top of the index, because the school averages all the scores of athletes on their teams. Other kids who can play really well may not have high grades and scores, so the coaches will usually only take kids from elite private schools with very high scores and grades because the private-school kids tend not to be the best players. The kids I work with don't always have these grades and scores, so they can't meet the Ivy League index no matter what they do. Their parents' donations are therefore a surer route to admission.

Nonetheless, New York is a land of arcane sports, played to get kids into elite colleges. Brooklyn is in particular a hive of squash activity. Parents join an exclusive club in Brooklyn Heights just by the East River called the Heights Casino. This institution, housed in a beaux arts building, has squash courts and pros (despite its name, it does not have gambling—a casino in the old days was a social club), and parents see these lessons as the ticket for their kids to enter the Ivy League—the one place in America, aside from suburban Connecticut, where squash is valued. Some are able to play their way into elite colleges, as not that many Americans have access to squash courts. Squash has become almost a religion among the elite of Brooklyn Heights, an area that while it is in Brooklyn, resembles the Upper East Side in its privilege and preppiness. It is the home to many bankers who are just one subway stop from Wall Street, and their kids play squash. They play it endlessly, so that kids on their way to school have squash rackets poking out of their bags. They play in the dawn and dusk hours, and they have squash coaches, many of whom are from Egypt, a legacy of English colonialism. Others travel to Egypt to play—or used to, before the Arab Spring. At the height of the unrest, when crowds were protesting en masse in Tahrir Square, one Brooklyn parent even complained to me, clucking, "The revolution is giving Egyptian kids an unfair advantage by closing their schools. They simply have more time to practice squash!" Some kids regularly travel to Yale, where there is a major tournament. These kids spout their national rankings like another kid might talk about what he has on his Spotify playlist.

At best, kids react to the stress of being subjected to constant competition by playing video games. At worst, like Trevor, they become reckless, trying to throw away the lives their parents have so carefully constructed for them. They take risks that are not motivated by anything other than the underlying need to self-destruct. Trevor, who tells me most things that are on his mind, informs me that he is addicted to smoking pot, and through sports, he befriends older kids who can supply it to him. Soon, he is—as he puts it—helping his friends, working as the middleman in drug transactions and making extra cash that he keeps in his desk and plans to invest in marijuana stocks. He assures me that to make his drug deals he is using a text function that the police cannot trace.

"Do you really think that text function is untraceable?" I ask him, choosing for a minute to ignore the larger problems around what he is doing.

"Blythe, Blythe, Blythe, yes! It absolutely is," he says, drawing his hands to his face, feigning disbelief that I could possibly think the NYPD could outwit a teenager.

"I wouldn't bet on it," I tell him.

"Oh my god! Yes, it is. All the drug dealers use it. Blythe, you don't know what you're talking about!"

We go around in circles like this for a few minutes, and I get nowhere.

When I insist on telling his parents about what he's doing, he is only momentarily angry with me. It seems that underneath all the bravado, he wants someone to stop him from self-destructing during his junior year of high school. I dread making the call to his father. Trevor's father receives my news about his son with a sober "Thank you," and that is the last I hear of it. He feels no need to discuss it with me. The matter will be handled internally.

I am surprised that Trevor faces no real consequences as a result of this situation. His father is strangely permissive when it comes to matters other than sports. It's as if nothing else matters, and he will excuse his son's stint as a wannabe-kingpin as long as Trevor stays on the path to the Ivies.

This widespread lack of parental discipline shows up in the classroom, too. When I was teaching at an exclusive private school, I was once taunted by a group of sophomore boys. "Are you a stewardess?" they asked me because

I was wearing a Tibetan scarf. I'm not even sure why they connected a scarf with being a stewardess (though I guess some stewardesses wear them, but so do their Fifth Avenue mothers). They clearly enjoyed placing me, their teacher, in a less dominant status. When I tried to keep teaching, they burst out, one after the other:

"Can you get me nuts?"

"Can you pour me a soda?"

"Where's my beer?" There was a lot of laughter, riotous at times.

The kids were not laughing the next day when I subjected them to a surprise reading quiz and told them I would give a quiz day after day until they shaped up. Many responded, incredulously, "But you can't do this to us, Dr. Grossberg!" I received many emails from parents complaining that their sons were not to blame and were being targeted unfairly. There wasn't one parent or student who supported me or sent an email of apology, but the kids eventually learned to give me some grudging respect (perhaps only for my stubborn streak, which can be quite extreme) and learned something about history (and possibly how to treat others).

There are many kids who live in a zone in which their only responsibilities are school and sports. Like Trevor, Alex has spent more of his life on the playing fields than in his bed. In the afternoons, a black SUV arrives at his private school and whisks him away to private tennis lessons. He's too good to play on his school's mediocre team, and he needs the daily contact with his coach. He plays for several hours after school, and sometimes rises in the dawn hours to play before as well. His coaches look at every aspect of

his play, and he is nationally ranked. He knows his ranking, and he shares it freely with others.

In rain, sleet, and snow, Alex's driver, an immigrant from
Puerto Rico, is determined to get his charge to practice.
The driver nervously taps the steering wheel in traffic and
listens to salsa, turned way down so he doesn't disturb his
passenger, while Alex plays video games on his phone in
the back seat. Alex's mother even insisted that her son attend tennis practice when school was canceled and the city
was shut down for a week by Hurricane Sandy. Fortunately,
the tennis club had electricity when much of the city had
lost power. Alex doesn't remember when, or if, he made the
decision to play this sport, but he can't recall a time when
earning a national ranking in tennis hasn't been his destiny.
When practice is over at 7:00 p.m., the Escalade glides up
to the club to return Alex safely to his Park Avenue apartment building. He spends far more time with his driver
than with his parents, who often don't come home until
long after I've tutored Alex in writing. While we write,
he slices the air with an imaginary racket, as if his mind
is never off the courts. Even when he is at his computer, I
can see him hunching his shoulders, wiping the sweat off
his nose, readying himself for the next volley.

Despite spending most of his life in the Escalade, Alex
has a quick mind. He doesn't say much, but when we speak
about post–World War II suburbanization, he can write sen-
tences like "Suburbanization accelerated after the war, moving more privileged people out of cities." He immediately
grasps the connection between the growth of highways and
suburbs and white flight without my explicitly explaining it

to him, and he has a clear, effortless writing style. Looking at his inscrutable face, I can't tell how he knows so much. He is, like Owl Eyes in *The Great Gatsby,* a person who sees and intuits a great deal, even if he doesn't look up from his gaming console.

Every moment in Alex's day is parsed and exploited. In the hours he is not playing tennis with his private coach, he is traveling to tournaments, or working with his Yale-educated math-and-science tutor. He also has a separate SAT tutor who charges $800 an hour and who has helped him strategize about every aspect of the test, down to where he'll sit in the room and the snacks he'll eat between sections.

He also has a few psychiatrists who help him manage his anxiety. The levels of anxiety among all kids has skyrocketed in recent years, the result of constant contact with others and social media on their smartphones. The rates of anxiety among rich kids rivals that of the poorest kids in the nation. They contend with very different stressors, but they face the kinds of insecurity that people find unsettling. The poor don't know where or how they are going to live or pay for what they need, or whether they are going to be safe walking home. The rich don't know where they stand or how they measure up, or if someone loves them for their own sake. Their stresses are very real to them, though perhaps they don't seem pressing to others. Alex's doctors also spend a great deal of time speaking with his parents, who are worried about his apathy, and helping him strategize about his schoolwork and about his standardized testing.

Though his parents are very wealthy and he could live for the rest of his life on the money they plan to give him, they feel it's very important that he be admitted to a top-notch college, which means the Ivy League. It's complicated figuring out why Harvard, Yale, and Princeton (*HYP* in admissions parlance) mean so much to rich parents. For poor parents, admission to this type of college means a path to a totally different life for one's child. For rich parents, it's more about wanting a return on investment—all the time and resources they put into their kids will have paid off if they lead to this type of college. And of course, in this era, when people post their college-admission results on social media, it is sweet to have bragging rights to an HYP admission. It's likely the same reason people take pictures of the entrées in their pricey restaurant dinner and post them online. They want to make other people envious. The parents, who are from Philadelphia's Main Line, are also wary of any sign of slippage in status—that they are no longer at the top. Alex's parents are hoping for Harvard or Yale, but University of Pennsylvania might be the most likely, as his parents are alumni. As a legacy, or the child of alumni, he has a leg up in the admissions process. For example, Brown admits about a third of legacy children, but only about 13 percent of other applicants. Other Ivy League schools have similar rates of legacy admissions—at Harvard, legacies are admitted at more than five times the rate of other students.

He plays video games on his phone in the SUV on the way to practice, and he doesn't need to do any of his schoolwork on his own. He waits for his tutor to do it. All his needs are taken care of, and dinner is waiting when he gets home. His room is picked up and cleaned, and his cleaned clothes are magically returned to his drawers. He has never been food shopping in his life, but he knows how to order food to be delivered. He speaks to few people, save his tennis coach, though he has started to meet up with some of the kids at school to vape nicotine. He does that during his free times at school, as all his after-school hours are busy. He's gotten to sixteen at this breakneck speed, and though he has been diagnosed with depression, he's not aware of feeling particularly depressed.

Alex is too anesthetized and controlled to feel anxiety. He doesn't have a moment to breathe, and all the uncertainty of life has been removed from his path—mainly. He doesn't have to think, and any time he can slip away from his parents and their schedules, he delves into various kinds of anesthesia—first playing video games and later smoking pot. He hasn't thought enough about his situation to realize he is depressed. That might come later.

Like Trevor, he becomes a heavy consumer of marijuana and he's discovered smoking it in the tennis club. The coach makes a call home to Mom, who already knows her son smokes pot but thinks evil classmates feed it to him. What she hasn't realized is that he is also stealing. She keeps money lying around the apartment—thousands of dollars at times—and some of the money is missing. She tends to be sloppy about the amounts she stuffs in drawers, so she doesn't realize at first that Alex has been slipping hundreds of dollars into the pockets of his designer jeans. She pumps her son until she gets out of him why he's taking the money and where he's spending it.

Though Alex lives in the most dynamic city in the world, his world is small, and he interacts in very limited ways with the people of New York. Rather than going out to the city, the city has, throughout his life, come to him, in the form of baby nurses, nannies, housekeepers, cleaners, tutors, chefs, coaches, trainers, and others who visit them at home. His home is his world, and the private school he attends is a home away from home, a secluded place that is similarly upscale.

These kids don't get much time to breathe, and they certainly don't spend a lot of time in their rooms. When I was growing up, I spent so much time staring at my ceiling that I think I knew every swirl. There were a lot of afternoons, during the summer in particular, that I spent reading or sleeping or dreaming. These kids don't have time for that, and they don't have the inclination either, as they are always on their phones. Of course that's true of a lot of middle- and upper-middle-class kids in America today, too. But there's something steroidal about the way the very rich in Manhattan and Brooklyn fill their time.

What are the practical side effects of these types of activities? Certainly sleep deprivation. Certainly anxiety, and often depression. The anxiety and depression among New York's elite children have a certain palpability. Experts believe that the children of the affluent suffer twice as much depression as the kids in the South Bronx or East New York who are struggling just to get to school safely and help their parents keep a roof over their heads. It doesn't make sense, but the findings are robust. Kids like Alex, Trevor, and Lily are hothouse flowers, who are propped up by their parents and support staff but who know that they can't measure up.

Their parents drag them toward college, and then it's any-body's guess how they'll handle the rest of their adult lives with the sense of not measuring up.

The research of Suniya S. Luthar, Co-Founder & Chief Research Officer at Authentic Connections and professor emerita at Teachers College at Columbia, has exposed the risks of affluence. While the conventional wisdom is that children with high socioeconomic status are at little risk of developing substance-abuse disorders, anxiety, and depression, research suggests otherwise. Children of affluent parents are in fact at higher risk for these disorders than kids at the opposite extreme of the socioeconomic ladder.

Luthar and her colleagues believe that there are different "pathways," or explanatory factors, for the problems of affluent children. One, Luthar says, is achievement pressure imposed by parents who value accomplishments over personal qualities and whose children absorb this pressure. The other is isolation from adults, as affluent parents are less likely to spend time with their children, who are also more likely to be involved in after-school activities that erode family time. Eating dinner with just one parent on most nights has been shown to have a protective effect for children, but this is not the regular practice in many affluent homes. The children of Fifth Avenue are often home alone, and the attention they receive from their parents is often about achievement rather than other parts of their lives. Luthar has found that children among both the very wealthy and the very poor are likely to admire peers who defy authority.

Researchers, and perhaps the public at large, have long

taken it for granted that the higher the socioeconomic status, the greater the benefits, but Luthar asserts that in fact
the benefits taper off or even go down as one reaches the
top of the ladder. While there are many studies showing
that children with higher socioeconomic status, or SES,
do better in life, Luthar points out that they were largely
conducted on middle-class kids. Only now are researchers
like her dissecting these claims to figure out if more is less
and whether children can really have too much of a good
thing. The highest levels of affluence tend to be accompa-
nied by a pressurized lifestyle that, in Luthar's research, has
been shown to predict problems among children.

Alex, like many children in the top 1 percent, is more
likely to use drugs and alcohol than children in other economic classes. Luthar has followed wealthier children well
into their twenties and has found that by age twenty-six,
they are two to three times more likely to have been diagnosed with a substance-abuse problem. Affluent kids are
more likely to binge-drink and more likely to abuse Ritalin
and party drugs like cocaine and Ecstasy. Luthar believes
that kids use these drugs to cope with the pressures of the
expectations that parents have for them. She contends that
there are many pathways that lead to problems in communities that place a high emphasis on achievement.

"It's a survival-of-the-fittest mentality," she says. "While
kids in the inner city truly compete to see who will make
it out alive, kids in high-achieving schools also have this
type of mentality and think, 'There are only a few choice
colleges or careers. My loss is your gain, your gain is my
loss'," Luthar says.

Her work shows that kids continue to use substances into college and that parents may look the other way because they are more concerned with their children's academic performance. Alex's parents take his drug use seriously, however, and they bring him to a psychiatrist, who finds that Alex is mum, unresponsive, and unable to open up about what's on his mind.

Among many affluent children, there is also a sense of entitlement so massive that it could sink the *Titanic*. It's as if they fear that they don't really measure up, and entitlement fills the crevices in their souls. There's nothing quite like a white boy who has attended an elite New York private school and who hasn't gotten wise to his place in the world and how it was made possible. Some of the students I taught at one Manhattan private school even believed in social Darwinism—the discredited idea that one is rich because one is better, simply stated. They defended it with all their hearts. One unabashed sophomore from Park Avenue explained it to me. "We're here because our parents were just smarter and more athletic than other people's parents." I liked the addition of "more athletic" and still do, though this boy was entirely clumsy.

At first, though I can sense my students' corrosive anxiety, it doesn't corrode my life. Sure, I worry when they have too much to do or tell me that they stayed up until 3:00 a.m. or have a volleyball championship in Rhode Island that is going to interfere with studying for finals. But their lives don't cause me to toss and turn at night and wake up with a sick feeling in my stomach, until I start getting late-night calls myself.

Like, for example, the 9:30 p.m. call I get from Sophie's mother. "Sophie likes you," she tells me, in her raspy Long Island voice with the din of a restaurant in the background. "She's upset about her biology test. Can you call her? She's been crying all night."

I call Sophie, and I can tell she's just upset because she's had the typical hormone-infused roller-coaster day of an exhausted teen who needs someone to speak to at night. "I got a B− on the bio test," she sobs. "And I worked soooo hard." She goes on to produce a litany of complaints, including "my friends didn't invite me to brunch" and "my English teacher bullies me." In her conception of the world, most behavior she doesn't like, including the assignment of homework, constitutes bullying. After issuing a string of incriminations that characterize most of the people in her world as bullies, including her best friend's mother who insists her daughter return home by 11:00 p.m., Sophie rapidly recovers and rings off, telling me she has to study for a math quiz the next day. I realize she just needed to talk and her mother outsourced it to me. Her parents throw themselves into socializing with the exhaustive zeal they give to every other aspect of their lives, and they aren't there for her. Her cries echo into the empty white apartment and drop on her perfectly positioned Limoges boxes made out of fancy French porcelain with golden springs. Another time Sophie sprains her ankle on an overnight school trip, and the teacher who is chaperoning can't get her parents to answer their cell phones. After the teacher drives Sophie to an emergency room in upstate New York and then back home, her parents explain that they were at a business function that they just couldn't interrupt.

Eventually, Sophie also gets in trouble. I only learn about it when her mother calls to ask me to write a letter to a judge explaining why Sophie hasn't been able to do a lot of after-school activities because she has needed so much tutoring. I admire the way her mother can phrase everything so neatly. The judge questioned why Sophie wasn't a better citizen and wasn't involved in community work, and her mother wants me to explain that Sophie has had to use her after-school time for tutoring.

"Sophie had an incident," she explains. "I think her friend egged her on to do it. Anyway, she only stole two things, but the store wanted to make an example of her. She's always liked you," her mother says. This is always her way to get me to do things because she knows I'm a softy, easily manipulated because I want to help her daughter. "I'll give you instructions from Sophie's lawyer about the kind of letter I need from you. We need it by next week."

The letter I write functions as a kind of character statement for Sophie and is intended to show the judge that she is a good citizen. Sophie decided to shoplift some items from a very exclusive department store, and it turns out that they don't take shoplifting lightly. She selected only a few items, including diamond stud earrings, but their total cash amount was not a joke to the department store, and they are pressing charges. Using the template provided by the lawyer, I write a letter that includes the school she attends and the learning issues she has, as well as the number of hours I work with Sophie each week. I think of those perfectly aligned Limoges boxes in her room and the number of nights she has spent at home with only her dogs and her housekeepers. What was she actually trying to steal from that store? Was it attention and love? I wait for Sophie to bring up her arrest and subsequent community-service requirement with me, but she never does.

In a world where parents are at ballet benefits or in Paris on a typical Wednesday night, I'm more than just a tutor. In a world that rises and falls on grades, SAT scores, college admissions, and squash rankings, every minute of action the kids take seems to acquire outsize importance. What doesn't seem to attract as much attention is their lives as kids, as people who need someone to talk to at the end of the day, as people who sometimes have acne.

Still, I am not crushed by heartache until I meet Ben, the sixteen-year-old who lives in a tony hotel room, where similar ones rent for almost a thousand dollars a night. His parents live in a room nearby with a younger brother, but they are never home. His father has legal problems that forced him to sell their Upper East Side brownstone, and his foreign-born mother travels to play golf as an amateur. He doesn't have a kitchen, but his mother slips a note under his door that says *Order dinner. I'm going out*, so he can have his choice from the room-service menu. His favorite dish is the signature hotel burger on a ciabatta roll for twenty-seven dollars, served with a linen napkin rolled in a silver ring.

His room has the uninhabited, swept-clean look of most hotels, and the only personal touch he has been able to import from the brownstone where he once lived is his video-game console. The room is neatened each day by the attentive housekeeping staff, so the touches he leaves on the room are removed. Even the menu is carefully propped up in its place, as is the housekeeping notice about conserving towels. The only thing on his desk is a card from the therapist he has just seen, a PhD on the Upper East Side of Manhattan. His sports gear is not in evidence, perhaps stashed in a closet, and only his backpack and a few pairs of sweatpants clutter his duvet cover.

The counselor at Ben's Manhattan private school asks me to work with him, as he struggles to write about the sophisticated literature he is studying. Bereft of parental supervision, Ben spends his days shuttling between his allergist and therapist and ordering room service.

He often goes to school without the proper clothes on because his parents forget to go shopping for him. While his mother is always seen wearing designer clothes, he showed up for his school's field day wearing a ripped T-shirt while other kids wore the requisite, neat polo shirts. His mother is everywhere—at society events, looking more and more pinched each time, and in the Hamptons in the summer. She is never home.

The routine details of her children's lives are not her domain. The hired staff at the hotel look in on the boy when they can, and they act nervous around him, as if their jobs depend on his satisfaction. When I arrive to tutor him, we work in the small business center that overlooks a dark cocktail lounge, where crooners who headlined in Las Vegas in the '70s now sing. The business center doesn't have a door, implying that no one really comes to the hotel to do work but rather to soak up the atmosphere. When he orders an orange juice, it comes with a maraschino cherry and a sword-shaped toothpick in a cocktail glass, as if a drink can't depart from the bar without wearing the guise of alcohol. He takes a cab to school, without anyone to see him off and make sure he has his homework and gym clothes. No one says anything—no one at his private school on the Upper East Side, no one at the hotel. They are all too well paid.

He doesn't crack *The Great Gatsby*, though it was assigned to him, but he is suddenly and unexpectedly enthusiastic about *As I Lay Dying*, Faulkner's absurdist tale of the fruitless quest of the Bundrens, a down-and-out Southern family, to bury their mother. Ben is laconic, sedate by nature. During my tutoring sessions with him, he lets entire passages of *The Great Gatsby* wash over him with no comment, as if the American dream and its cracks don't apply to his crumbling family. But somehow, the Bundrens, separated from Ben by the geographic and cultural distance between Manhattan and Yoknapatawpha County, appeal to him.

"I love the Bundrens!" he says in a rare moment of happiness. His face registers a flickering grin, and then he retreats back into his shell and his world. At the end of the school year, after earning the highest grade of his junior year on his Faulkner paper, he departs for the Hamptons.

Another boy whose situation caused me to lose sleep lived in his apartment by himself. His parents were divorced, and his father worked in another city during the week. The family had bought the son's former babysitter a studio apartment in the same building so she would be nearby if he needed an adult, but he was still, at age sixteen, alone most nights of the week. There are many kids like him, alone in the city because their parents are out in the Hamptons, or because their parents have to travel so much that they don't even know which city they will be in at night.

These kids are, like Gatsby himself, not entirely at home in their own homes. When Nick is touring Gatsby's mansion, he observes, "His bedroom was the simplest room of all—except where the dresser was garnished with a toilet set of pure dull gold." The innermost chambers of the house, where few guests go, are unadorned because everything is simply for show.

5

Freud on Fifth Avenue

On a drowsy winter's morning, I sit on the subway to Manhattan from Brooklyn, happy to have found a seat, and crack open a fresh print copy of the New York Times. To have a chance to read the paper on the subway is surreally wonderful since I can rarely sit, and I curl my toes in anticipation.

There, on the front page, is Sophie's father, in a pinstriped suit and shielding himself from photographers by holding, coincidentally, a *New York Times* in front of his balding head. I put the paper down, my heart pounding, not sure if I can read on, but I do. He has been charged with financial wrongdoing, and he is being investigated.

I have to go to Sophie's house that afternoon to tutor. Approaching her building, I run through multiple ways I can broach the subject. Do I simply ask how she's feeling? Do I wait for her to bring up the issue? Do I just jump right into the Opium Wars in China, which she is studying? I've never been in this situation before, as I never confronted her about her shoplifting incident, and I want to follow her lead.

When I ring the doorbell, there are yapping dogs, as always. The Filipino housemaid takes my coat and tells me Sophie's in her room. I find her lying upside down on her bed, blaring music, just a bit louder than usual.

Without greeting me, she yells, at the top of her lungs, "Mom! Blythe's here!" She tells me, "My mom wants to talk to you." She hums along to her music and then goes into her private bathroom. Her mother, Maria, whisks into the room, trailing perfume, the gold bangles on her wrist clattering. I steel myself for the talk ahead and prepare myself to say, "I'm sorry. If there is anything I can do…" or whatever someone is supposed to say in these moments, when another's loved one is accused of financial impropriety and the news is splashed across the *New York Times*.

"Oh, Blythe, good," Maria says. "I just wanted to let you know that Sophie received a B+ on her French Revolution paper. Not sure what went on there." She scans the paper and traces it with her red lacquered nails. "Oh, here it is. The teacher said to use more primary sources, so if you could help Sophie with the rewrite…."

I'm dumbfounded, speechless. "Sure," I mumble.

Sophie comes out of the bathroom, and she looks more subdued than before. We work together without making any unnecessary chitchat. I keep waiting for the right moment to acknowledge the elephant in the room, and I feel it pass between us, like high waves off Montauk. I keep thinking she'll say something, or that I will, but we don't.

I finally understand that she doesn't want to talk about it. She just wants me there, as I'm there every Wednesday, to establish some routine in her life, and we leave it at that. It is never mentioned between us.

Her English teacher calls me to chat about Sophie, and he says, "I knew her father was doing something wrong."

"But how could you have known that?" I ask him.

"Because people who are that rich are always doing something to get an advantage. How can they do better than everyone else? Because they break the law." I think about this observation endlessly over the next few days, months, years. I'm not quite sure what to think. On the surface, it seems to have a certain veracity to it, but I don't know for sure. I would like to believe it's not true.

While Sophie's family is going through these travails, about which she is entirely silent, they decide to sell their apartment. "We're nomads," her mother declares histrionically, as they move into a luxury hotel suite for a while as they search for a new apartment. As it turns out, Sophie is in good company. Another family (not Ben's) from her school lives down the hall while their house is being fixed up. They are simply renovating their Upper West Side brownstone, which looked so good beforehand that it was featured in a national magazine. But they feel compelled to re-renovate a few years later, tearing out their kitchen and building an ecofriendly exterior, so they, too, are nomads, for the time being.

Sophie's family turns with fresh energy to her grades and those of her younger brother, an apparently successful student who plays the violin. Even while her father mounts his defense, Maria is constantly at Sophie's school. When Sophie receives another B on a history paper, Maria bypasses the teacher and marches into the office of the Upper School head. She has asked me to join this meeting. "Sophie has simply never gotten these types of grades," Maria tells the head. "I think the teacher and she must have gotten off on the wrong foot because our Sophie is a bit politically conservative for this school."

The head and I look at each other, and he takes the paper and looks it over, his bristling eyebrows moving up and down as he reads. "I'm not sure that this grade is reflective of political differences," he says. "She didn't format her sources correctly, and she hasn't read deeply enough into her primary source."

It's now time for Sophie's mother to use the legal card. "You know, this is a difficult time for our family," she begins, her voice catching. "You would think that an educator at this type of school could afford some type of courtesy to Sophie. She has always been a stellar student. As I said, she has never gotten this type of grade before."

Sophie's mother should be on her husband's defense team. Sophie is allowed to redo her paper, and soon after, her father is fined what, for him, is a meaningless amount of money. He avoids jail time, and she gets an A− in the class. Still, her mother remains worried.

During the last session of the school year, she pulls me aside. "As you know," she tells me, "next year is a really big one for Sophie, junior year. Do you think she's ready?"

"Yes," I say. "She has made some good strides this year. She reads well, pen in hand, and is ready to really think about whether her evidence supports what she is trying to say."

"Well, I'm not sure. I'm troubled by what her teacher says." Sophie's mother plucks her daughter's paper off her granite countertop. The paper is so wrinkled it's clear that her mother has gone over it countless times, tracing each and every word with her red lacquered nails. "She says that Sophie is still not digging deeply enough and that her ideas could be better sequenced. Is this something that you, Blythe, could help her with?"

I don't know how to respond to this. I've worked with Sophie on ordering her ideas, but I can only work with what she comes up with. I find it surprising that Maria is questioning me about basics after two years of tutoring. "Of course," I say simply. "Of course."

"Well, we'll be in the Hamptons starting next week. When do you come out East?"

"Well, I don't," I tell her.

"Do you go to Fire Island, then?"

"No, I don't. I stay here and go to Massachusetts, where my parents live, for a week."

"So no plans to come out East, huh?" Maria is uncharacteristically stumped, incredulous that I don't leave the city all summer. "We'll just have to get you out there. Or maybe Skype. Could she Skype with you after tennis?"

"Yes, of course. We can work on her fall reading." Relief spreads over her mother's face, akin to the relief she likely felt when her husband avoided jail time, I imagine. "Great, Blythe. We'll Skype, then." She pats my hand.

As Freud, who understood neuroses so well, might have predicted, the fear exhibited by Maria runs rampant among the New York elite, in spite of their increasing opulence. The reality of the neo-gilded age in which we live is that the top 1 percent, and especially the top .01 percent, own more than ever before. They have a near stranglehold on the nation's goods and wealth, and their share of the wealth is only increasing, while the rest of us watch our wealth fall or stagnate. But their *perception* of their place in the world is very different, and they believe that if they don't exercise constant frenetic competitiveness, they will fall. Their wealth has the ironic effect of not calming them down but making them evermore restless.

The old gilded age was filled with men and women who spent the summers eating boned fowl and turbot in lobster sauce and yachting in Newport, but the neo-gilded age is filled with men and women who don't stop working and fretting. They bring their cell phones and iPads on their sailboats. This isn't rare, even among the middle class, but the elite supercharge their work with a kind of hyperactivity that extends to every aspect of their lives.

The elite in the gilded age weren't afraid of outside threats because there didn't seem to be any. They were instead afraid of a kind of weakness from within, a corruptive, corrosive softness that they thought would cause their class to putrefy. As a result, their children's schools were marked by austere conditions and tough headmasters. Perhaps the most notorious at that time was Groton School (which now bears no resemblance to its earlier, Spartan self) under its founding headmaster, Reverend Endicott Peabody. He was himself an embodiment of the "muscular Christianity" he advocated and was not afraid of going door-to-door in Tombstone, Arizona, to raise funds for a new Episcopal church only shortly after the notorious gunfight at the O.K. Corral. In the early days of Groton, the students, all boys, were permitted to take only cold showers, and they were not allowed to receive more than twenty-five cents a week in allowance, even though they were from some of the richest families in the country.

Clinton Trowbridge, who attended Groton in the early 1940s, writes about receiving disciplinary "blackmarks" that meant he had to run around the track surrounding the Circle, the grounds at the center of the school, for six hours—*six hours!* For worse infractions, students were sentenced to "black death," a punishment in which they were locked in a room for three days with bread, water, and a Bible for sustenance.

It's impossible to imagine parents—not to mention state authorities—countenancing this type of punishment now. Today's private schools do not follow the Spartan mantra. They are appointed with rugs, chandeliers, and comfy libraries in which kids can sleep in leather chairs. The dining services in many schools serve gourmet food, and there are festive holiday meals with artisanal hot chocolate. While they don't all have field houses, most private schools in New York City have gyms with fitness equipment, dance studios, choral rooms, and state-of-the-art chemistry labs. In addition, their discipline is lax in that the worst they generally have kids do is stay after school or come early.

But schools are allowed to do what their parents permit, and today, while corporal and unreasonable punishments are not allowed, schools often push students to their psychological limits. The Spartan element of today's schools comes from the classes themselves. They are far more rigorous than those of yesteryear, and perhaps the cold showers at Groton in Peabody's time would be preferable to many students. In one school, kids read *The Odyssey*—one of the unabridged translations—in middle school. In high-school history classes, students are expected to have already mastered the conventional narrative of history so that they can dive into analyzing primary sources, such as the Cherokee Constitution and William Jennings Bryan's "Cross of Gold" speech. These are documents written decades, if not centuries, ago, and they require considerable patience for students to unravel. In many cases, kids simply don't have the context to read them, but some private-school teachers feel that they should have this grounding. Therefore, the teachers don't provide background, and the students are on their own. In math classes, there are students who are several years ahead of the typical math sequence, meaning that they're well beyond the standard calculus curriculum by senior year and take classes through online consortiums and at universities. Students who aren't at this advanced level feel lacking and can't keep up. At the same time, they are expected to delve into extracurricular activities, to become part of the currents of activism sweeping across schools. There are clubs for LGBTQ+ students, for Latinx students, for feminists (male and female), for biracial people, for Asians, for Jews, and for all manner of interests. In short, students are stretched to their limits. While school brochures make this type of enrichment sound exhilarating, it is nothing short of exhausting much of the time, for parents, students, and teachers alike.

Class discussions can be intense and tend to favor students who feel comfortable jumping in and expressing themselves. Some kids like William, the boy who objected to the idea that one's social class affects one's view of money, are adept at monopolizing discussions. William is confident to the point of brashness, or appears so, and he combs the newspaper to have statistics ready to prove his point. He tends to talk over people and to interrupt, and he has a way of shutting others down.

He is not alone, and it's hard for people who are less confident or verbally facile to get into the conversational mix. At one meeting of the liberal political group at a private school I work at, the conversation is supposed to be run in popcorn style. That means students speak and choose the next speaker. I watch one boy after another call on other boys, even while speaking about feminism, so that there are virtually no female voices in the room. One girl is finally called on, and she chooses to call next on a boy. Some girls have their hands up, but many sit in silence, bored looks on their faces. Students of color are also quiet, and most don't even have their hands up during this meeting of the liberal club.

Kids who have language-based learning disorders, such as Sophie, can also be left out of the conversation. It's hard to know whether Sophie doesn't care to participate or whether it's just been so hard for her to voice her opinions quickly that she has long ago given up. Teachers constantly remark on her silence in class, and they suggest that she jump into the conversation. This remark appears so often in teachers' boilerplate comments on her report card that she has come to discount it.

The irony is that at home, Sophie speaks a lot. The older child of two, she speaks over her younger brother and is constantly arguing with her parents. It's as if all her verbal energy is expended at home, as she's silenced at school. Still, at the end of the day, it's hard to tell what she cares about. She is infected by the bug of popular culture and reads online about her favorite celebrities. She can spend hours surfing the web and is up to date about the younger Kardashians on a daily level, while she is not as well versed in her classwork.

The cult of celebrity affects most of the kids I work with. It's like they have, through osmosis, learned everything about reality TV, and they make constant references to reality stars as if they are friends. These personalities are known mainly for being personalities, and their activities absorb the kids I work with. Parents know about them, too, and conversation centers around people who do nothing but elevate themselves for doing nothing. The idea is that one is a brand name and has to keep constantly in the media and on social media. While most American kids celebrate celebrities, the 1 percent can emulate their lives, so their connection is perhaps a bit more intimate. They work with them or have at least encountered them before. When a celebrity or sports figure like former Yankees player Derek Jeter comes up in the classroom, a student is bound to say she's met him or that he lives in her building and she saw him in the elevator in the morning.

The kids are the center of their own minimedia campaigns. In addition to having social-media accounts, some students have online school accounts that tell their parents everything that their children are doing. While Lily's mother runs an entire division of a bank, she still has time to microanalyze each of her daughter's assignments and to arrive home, thanks to her daughter's school website, knowing exactly what her daughter should be doing. She knows when her assignments are due and what's coming up next week. When she gets home at 9:30 p.m., she often peppers her daughter with questions about her grades and assignments before heading overseas on an early-morning flight. Lily's mother keeps in touch from France and doesn't let an ocean interfere with her daily involvement in her daughter's schoolwork.

She often calls from overseas, and I think surely, she must have left a negotiating table to phone me. Is Angela Merkel waiting in the other room for her banker to get off the phone? She mentions calling Lily's school several times, and I momentarily feel like an awful parent: I am not as involved in my seven-year-old's school as she is in Lily's high school, even though I never leave New York. I simply don't know how she does it.

I always feel second-rate when I am with Lisa. She somehow manages to get her nails done every weekend, even though she is constantly traveling. And she is never late. When I am ten minutes late because there was a subway rerouting on a Sunday and I had to take three subways and run across Houston Street to get from Brooklyn to Manhattan, she says to me, "I notice you're a bit late these days."

"It was track work," I tell her.

"The track work? What's that?" she asks. I forget that Lisa is one of the few New Yorkers who never takes a subway. She uses a private driver, and the phrase *track work*, so immediately understood by most of the other 8.5 million New Yorkers, means absolutely nothing to her. Everyone else accepts that one is late because of track work because it is the maze through which they must travel each day, particularly on Sundays, when there is additional track work. No one questions the veracity of this statement, except Lisa.

"You know, they are working on the subway lines, so there are delays," I explain. "I had to take three subways to get here, and I had to wait twenty minutes."

"Oh, the subway. I took the subway the other day. Everyone was looking at me, wondering what I was doing there." She is still clearly miffed by the track work excuse and doesn't quite believe it.

Though parents on Park Avenue are intensely concerned with their children's grades, pimples, and squash scores, they are often away from home. While many of the women like Sophie's mom don't work—in spite of calling themselves *writers* because they wrote a piece for *New York* magazine in the early 1990s—they throw themselves into socializing and fundraising so that they are unlikely to see their children on any given day after school drop-off unless the school has a function on.

Freud's concept of pathological narcissism explains some of the parents I interact with, as their sense of self-worth relies on fleeting accomplishments, including those of their children. Fretting about appearances, they seem distanced from the actual emotional life of their kids. But it's more than that. It's fear that runs deep in their veins. Fear of failure, fear of falling. These parents, having achieved the apogee of success and wealth, have nowhere to go but down. That makes them scared for their children and fretful.

Is it better to be a wealthy parent than a parent who can look forward to better things for one's child? In that toss-up, I might choose to be the parent who knows that her child will lead a better life than she has—the nurse from Barbados whose daughter has a scholarship to college, or the bus driver from Ghana who knows that his son is going to be a computer programmer. In these cases, hope is fulfilled.

It's interesting that many of the parents I work with have decided that their hopes for their children are to have them replicate their own lives. Some of these parents are wealthy enough to provide an eternal revenue stream for their children, even a life of extreme comfort. One could imagine that these parents might hope for their children to be what their heart desires, whether it's a banker, a dancer, or a vet technician. However, I've found that rarely to be the case. Instead, their hopes are confined within the narrow domains of what they are, generally speaking. There is some sexism at work in that the boys of Fifth Avenue, with some notable exceptions, are shepherded into banking, law, and commercial real estate (recently there are some who have entered tech fields), while the girls have more latitude to pursue careers that are seen as feminine, including teaching young children, working in art museums, and being designers. The women are also encouraged to pursue traditionally male fields, such as banking, law, and medicine.

Fear is a lot of what drives these parents, and that is an understandable reaction for parents in today's world, which is reeling from political and economic shock waves. During the recession of 2009, it seems as though some of their worlds are about to topple with the implosion of Bear Stearns and the crisis in the real-estate market. School administrators are nervous about the declining fortunes of the parents, and one or two parents lose their jobs, but they tend to find new jobs quite quickly for the most part.

In this climate, I expect my tutoring business to slacken, but it doesn't. If anything, it picks up, and I receive far more referrals for new students than I can accommodate. It seems as though parents are more worried than ever, and they want their kids to have every advantage they can muster. Trevor tells me one day, "My dad has put a limit on my haircuts." Trevor has the kind of hairstyle that requires biweekly cuts at an expensive salon, but I don't see any other impact of the recession on the families I work with. There could, of course, be ripples beneath the surface, but they emerge from the recession intact and, in the years after, go on to become even wealthier as real-estate prices rebound with a vengeance. Many families sell their apartments to take advantage of the higher prices, and they are again nomads, floating between luxury apartments on the Upper East Side.

Still, fear is not a rational emotion, and I respect it, as a parent. No parent should have to confine his or her emotions to what is rational. Sometimes, I wonder how much I should give in to it. My son has provoked comments from the talkative but indirect woman who runs his preschool. He is clearly not on the same developmental path as most of the other kids, and I start to watch his milestone markers slip by without notching too many successes. It's horrifying as a new parent to consult those *What to Expect When You're Expecting* books and to know that, somehow, you've gotten off the normal-ish trajectory entirely.

At first, my son does not crawl. He kind of scoots around on his butt, making holes in his pants as he scoots across Tuscany during a trip when he is one. Then, he doesn't walk. We see all manner of experts, including a very unfriendly physiatrist (a doctor who works with the spine and nerves) who makes us wait for ninety minutes in her empty waiting room. She can't deduce anything specific, but she makes seemingly unconnected remarks, such as "He has a large head." When I ask her, "What is wrong with him?" she snaps back, "I don't know. But it's not my job to placate you." That remark has always stuck in my mind, and it makes me feel sympathetic toward parents looking for an answer, living in fear.

My son has physical therapy and learns how to walk when he is twenty-six months old. Years later, reading the papers of Hans Asperger, the Austrian physician who first described boys we would call mildly autistic (or as having Asperger's syndrome, as it used to be called), I realize that my son is a textbook—as much as any child is textbook—example of a kid on the spectrum. But parents are blind, even parents like me who are trained not to be, and my son's diagnosis comes when he has just turned five.

Having a son on the spectrum while working with the kids I do is a surreal experience. On one hand, I feel immense sympathy for those who really struggle and their parents. In the competitive race of parenting, I've long ago gotten off the track. While I hear my colleagues talk about going to their child's travel baseball games in Pennsylvania and my students attend competitive squash meets on the weekend, I feel happy if my son can manage to get to a trampoline park for a half hour of jumping. My son has no ribbons or trophies in his room, as Trevor does from soccer and Lily does from squash and Sophie does from swimming, and he doesn't have pictures of his friends' parties as Sophie does. He has a piece of paper for being a good citizen at his special-needs camp.

As time goes on, and Lily, Sophie, and Trevor are hurtled through the path of milestones—from their private-school admissions to their ACTs and SATs—my son, my husband, and I have stepped off the path into a world where milestones are all relative. That is, my son's teachers do not measure him against some mythical bell curve but against what he did yesterday, and his growth is marked by immense strides forward followed by incredible declines. He looks like he is doing well as an eleven-year-old, attending sleep-away camp and starting to learn how to ride a bike—when the next year brings horrible aggression that requires hospitalization. My husband and I have long ago slipped from the world of mainstream parenting concerns.

Unlike the world of private-school parents, who feel at times that they must remain competitive with other parents, the parents we meet through our son's school are universally friendly. It's a relief to speak to them about special schools, about finding babysitters, about getting to bowling alleys at 9:00 a.m. when they are uncrowded. They understand the sensation of watching the world go by around you without feeling a part of it. Through it all, I have the consolation of being with my husband, a rare person who combines brilliance (knowledge of Persian, Arabic, and Urdu, along with an uncannily good imitation of the Jerky Boys, and the ability to play anything on the piano) with immense patience.

So, on one hand, while I feel a great connection with the parents I work with whose children struggle and with the parents of the special-needs students I work with, I feel less and less in common with the parents in the general swim of parenting. There are surreal moments, such as the summer when my son is in the hospital for aggression and parents from the school I work at keep calling and emailing me, including over July Fourth weekend, to ask me to apply for accommodations on standardized tests. They want to ask the College Board for 100 percent extra time (essentially, double time) even though their kids receive 50 percent extra time at school as an accommodation for having learning differences, and I have to tell them that the College Board doesn't allow me to apply for accommodations that their children do not have at school. I hear about squash victories and space camps and Scholastic Key Awards when a victory to me is having my son sit long enough in a barber's chair to get his hair cut.

But still, the fear is the same. We're all afraid for our children—we just show it in different ways. The parents who fire me when their son fails to hand in his homework are afraid for him, as is Lily's mom, Lisa. She wants to spare her daughter the pain of dealing with the mean girls who make Lily's life hell.

In the end, the patience I try to develop for my son
(though I often fail) makes me want to know what moti-
vates each and every parent. I try to look for, and understand, the fear that drives them. Even meddlers don't bother
me much anymore. I prefer these parents to the parents who
have nothing to do with their kids. They are in there trying, and that's all anyone can ask of them.

At the same time, fear drives the parents to extremes, and
wealthy parents have the resources to be more extreme. I'm
not immune to fear, but I can stubbornly live alongside it.
How I've always made sense of life is forcing myself to go
through each day. Surreal as it might seem at dawn, it usually gets better by noon, and it's usually done its worst by
dusk. But I meet a bunch of parents who want to spare their
children all that. They want to get them out of the nause-
ating perseverance of daily troubles.

Take Dakota, a really sweet, rail-thin girl with riveting
eyes. Her mother, a single parent, is a successful artist who
wants to spare her daughter all the angst of eighth-grade-girl
drama. She also wants to spare her all the angst of teenagerdom while still keeping her daughter at a private school.
Her solution is to remove her daughter from the school and
take her away for extended periods to Rome so that her
daughter doesn't have to deal with any mean girls. I heartily believe in Rome. It's soothing to everyone's souls. But
it's not soothing for the eighth-grade girl who has to return
from la dolce vita to the jealous girls who become steroi-
dally mean when they see their former friend get whisked
to Rome for weeks at a time. Toting her daughter to Eu-
rope, treating her to afternoon gelati, taking her shopping

in Trastevere—all good things for the summer, but not for the semester. Dakota's mother wants a traveling companion, not a daughter, and she wants Dakota's life to be filled with magic that is more appropriate for a young adult than a fourteen-year-old.

I understand this desire to shield one's child, to keep them away from things that one can't control or predict. My son attends a number of schools, even special-needs schools, that, rather than helping him, instead compound disasters with disasters. In one Brooklyn public school, the teacher, a young man who is under twenty-five and who knows little about autism, greets me at the front door of the kindergarten classroom each day, starting during the second week of school, and recommends another public-school program to me. With each passing day, it's apparent that my son is slipping so far behind what he is expected to do to succeed in the world of high-stakes testing—testing that is all-important to this school because it's in a high-socioeconomic-status neighborhood. The teacher points out that my son's drawings are too abstract—he fills his paper with numbers and letters—and that he should learn to make representational drawings. He points to a picture a girl has drawn of herself sitting with her family. It's far more adept than anything I could do, but it shows no individuality. My son learns to draw himself with a smile on his face, and we pass over that hurdle. Eight years later, he still draws himself this way. He even drew himself this way in the hospital.

I am not a confrontational person, so the summit we have at this public school, attended by the advocate we hire, is hellish for me. We ask for a paraprofessional to help my son.

The school responds with a flat no, and they tell me that they have sent his file to a coalition of private schools that can serve him. I realize later that this was the right move for everyone, but it takes years to find the right private school for him. Parents in this situation in New York City have to sue the board of education each year to get reimbursed for their child's special-education tuition (if they do not accept the public-school placement that is given to them), which can run over $80,000. It's not a scenario that I relish, but one that I have to accept.

I wondered at the time if I should argue with the school. Many of the parents I work with have, through force of will, been able to maintain their children at competitive private schools that simply aren't right for them. Sophie's parents have mastered the art of keeping up with all her classes and intervening when necessary. The online grade system allows them to see her results and to run interference with her teachers, if necessary. The family mounts a concentrated, savvy campaign to keep her afloat.

First, they give money to the school—a lot of money. Sophie's parents are close to the top donors in the school. Then, they give tickets they are not using to sports and arts events, like Knicks games and ballets, to the school to give away when they can't use them. They give teachers presents, big ones, though the school eventually decides that cash gifts are not allowed. During senior year, they buy the college counselors silk scarves and leave them on their desks so that they can't return them without it seeming very awkward. For routine efforts, such as the dean's help getting Sophie the homework she misses when she is on a cruise in

Venice, her parents send the dean an orchid in a porcelain pot. They tell Sophie's English teacher, "I'll make sure Sophie gives you a good rating on Rate My Teacher," a site on which students can submit public ratings and comments on their instructors.

When Sophie does not receive the grade she wanted, they can run a number of campaigns. They can enter the school with anger, or they can try to butter up the teacher. They often resort to anger when their demands are not met, and they use Sophie's father's legal trouble as a way to gain more advantages.

When Sophie was in middle school, she was not a solid student. She has ADHD, which has since been treated with a stimulant medicine, and she struggled with writing, though she has improved by working on a process with me and by meeting with her English teacher. There was talk of her leaving the school, which is consistently ranked among the best in the city, and that's when her parents truly brought their full-court press to the middle-school administration. There were several meetings. Sophie's mom asked to be CCed on all the emails from teachers to her daughter, in case Sophie did not read them, and Sophie was evaluated by a neuropsychologist. Because she was diagnosed with ADHD, she was given 50 percent extra time and the ability to take her tests in a distraction-free setting. She clearly needed these accommodations, and she has benefited from them. She has also worked with me as a private learning specialist, as she prefers not to work with the learning specialist in her school. The woman is one of the best learning specialists in the city—one who charges $200 an hour to do private work—but I understand that Sophie doesn't want to seem vulnerable at school, and her parents agree, not wanting other parents to know their daughter needs help.

Through all these efforts, Sophie has become a solid student in high school. She is not inspired, nor is she an intellectual, but she has stayed at her school and is now in the top 30 percent of her class. I marvel at her parents' energy and optimism, and I often wonder about my own son. Very rich parents have the resources to dedicate to their kids' advancement that I, working six days a week, do not, nor do most other parents. Should I have pushed harder for him to stay in a mainstream school, where he clearly was not getting everything he needed and where the teachers made it obvious that they did not want to work with him? Instead, he has entered the world of special-education schools, where the answer to which grade he is in is "I'm not really sure." His work is customized to him, and it often includes a large behavioral and social component. His experience is not comparable to those of kids in mainstream schools. Though I rationally know that I and most parents don't have the same resources to endlessly devote to their child, I still feel guilty about it.

Sometimes, the parents whose kids I work with ask me about my own child, and they seem to dread the answer, expecting that I will have a child who is academically perfect. When I tell them that my son has autism, I sometimes recognize it provides a sense of grim relief to them. The most charitable explanation is that they understand that we are all befuddled as parents. The least charitable, schadenfreude-ridden (though understandable) answer is that they take comfort in knowing that someone else's kid is worse off than their own. Overall, I find that the experience of being humbled as a parent is good for me. It makes me far less sure of what other parents should do except to continue to get involved with their children in loving ways.

When I'm standing by the sidelines at Trevor's soccer game or listening to Sophie sing or watching Lily play squash, I think how different my own son's childhood has been. And, yet, there is a commonality among all parents, riven with fear, wanting something better for our children and not knowing how to go about getting it.

6

The Lost Papers

When I was a young teacher, my students often told me that they lost their papers. Those who go to the Hamptons claim that they left their papers Out East on their other computers, though once Google Docs comes in, this is no longer possible (as documents are accessible through an email account in the cloud, not just through one computer). However, there are all manner of collapses even after the advent of Google Docs, including the implosion of students' Google accounts and the collapse of a school's Google Doc capabilities. Even in the digital age, the dog can still eat students' homework.

It's hard for me to assess these sudden disappearances, just as it is hard for me to understand at first the gaps in what parents tell me about the students I tutor. Many parents simply ask me to work with their kids without giving me the larger story. It is only after several years of working with Sophie, for example, that her mother casually mentions that Sophie was tutored for the ERB.

Julia, Trevor's cousin, is particularly difficult to figure out. Her parents hire me only to work with her in an AP American history class. They provide me with little context, though I've seen their summerhouse on the internet. It's really stunning, and I study the white sweep of the living room in hopes of understanding more about Julia and her family. I examine its gray-washed shingles, the side terrace where there is a breakfast area, and the kitchen with its shiny copper pots and elaborate range. On a real-estate website, I look at aerial photos of the expanse of the property and its amoeba-shaped pool. I am able to learn little from these photos. Often, I can gather quite a bit from going to a student's house, but Julia's Manhattan apartment and the online photos of the summerhouse on the ancestral island where Trevor's family also summers provide me with little insight. They are smooth, exactly as they should be, and nothing is personal about them. The only thing that sticks out to me is the photo Julia showed me of her black poodle lounging alongside the pool.

Julia wants to do well in this class. Her sophomore history teacher recommended that she not take it, but she likes history and wants to follow in her father's footsteps by studying it. Yet her essays are filled with errors, and she writes too little and has poor research skills. She busies herself in the thick scholarly books that she is assigned, books like Eric Foner's *A Short History of Reconstruction*, which perplexed me in college and would be formidable for any high-school student. There are endless footnotes in these books, and

names, and dates, and, in Foner's book, different phases of
Reconstruction and an overarching theory about why the
US government did not work to radically alter the condi-
tion of former slaves following the Civil War. It's difficult
material, but she lounges by her pool clad in a bikini and
makes her way through it even in the summer before she
takes the class as a way to get ahead in the reading.

During her junior year, she reads while other kids are
goofing around in the student lounge at her coed private
school. When she meets with me, she has annotated all of
her reading, marking the important passages and details.
She writes awkwardly, but her essays are full of details that
show she has read. Julia has a hard time jumping into class
discussions, and she is often tired. She fights for a B− each
semester and gets it, even though she spends a lot of time as
the captain of the girls' soccer team and receives far more
plaudits for that than for her academic work. She even meets
with me on a snow day. Once, just once, I find her in bed,
and she can't get out when I arrive at her apartment. One
of her housekeepers smiles at me, and says, "Jules has such
a hard time getting up. She is a lazy girl."

I don't think of Julia as lazy. Maybe she wants a few minutes to rest from the relentlessness of her day—the attention
and energy directed at her. She is seemingly never sad. Occasionally, her energy flashes into anger, and she is quick
to answer back to her parents and teachers. These moments
are just interruptions, staccato blips, in the generally posi-
tive flow of her energy. She is championed as a hero at her
school, where she is universally friendly, known for infectious laughter, and hardworking on the soccer field. Always

talking, she is the center of her social circle. In the rare free time she has, she teaches soccer clinics to younger kids and lets them climb on her until they tip her backward, her headband yanked free. The younger kids love her, calling out to her when she passes them in the hall, and she is kind enough to go over to talk to them.

She is always laughing, and she's quick to scurry off after going over the reading or working on her papers. In all the time I know her, I never have a very honest or heart-felt conversation with Julia, or Jules as her friends and her housekeeper call her. Despite all her talk, I know very little about her—something I realize when it is too late.

But I'm used to secrecy in its many forms, omissions and lies that expose themselves in ugly ways as my years of tu-toring go on. In another case, I get a call from Jonah's father when Jonah is in seventh grade. I've been recommended by the school as a writing tutor, and that's what we focus on. Jonah has not yet learned how to write a solid paragraph with a central claim, and he's not open to working on it.

Trying to get to three pages of writing on *To Kill a Mock-ingbird,* he admirably plops down a two-page-long passage from the book. When I ask him to pare it down to its es-sence, maybe a few essential lines, he chafes at the sugges-tion.

"My uncle is a publisher," he tells me. "And he knows more about publishing things than you do. He said it's okay." The two-page-long excerpt from the book remains.

I believe that Jonah has some fundamental language is-sues that could be cleared up from an evaluation, and I try to email his parents about my concerns several times but don't hear back anything definitive from them. Finally, at the end of the school year in June, his father, a very educated man who works as a lawyer, meets me at a downtown café and pays for my coffee as we chat. When I see he is reading a book by an author my husband likes, I mention that the author also wrote about the Caribbean, and he spends several minutes disagreeing with me, protesting that it can't possibly be true because he knows every book this author has ever written. I dismiss the subject and try to move on to Jonah. Initially, he seems receptive to the idea that his son might have a learning issue, and he says that he and his wife, who have ample resources, will have him evaluated.

When he gets home, he emails me, fulsome in his apologies that the author had in fact written about the Caribbean. He even refers to himself as having been sexist for having contradicted me and begs my forgiveness. I don't really focus on that but provide him with the contact information for several evaluators I like and trust. When I email him and his wife in the fall asking them to arrange the tutoring schedule for the following year, they tell me that the time slot I have for their son won't work because of his sports and that they are looking for someone else to work with him on writing. They tell me that they have not had him evaluated. That is the last I hear about them for two years, until I learn that Jonah has been suspended from school for distributing a list of girls he'd like to sleep with. He wasn't the only one involved in the infraction, but he doesn't return to the school.

I can't connect the dots fully from Jonah's seventh-grade learning issues to his tenth-grade suspension, but I have theories that can fill in the missing gaps. He fell further and further behind his classmates and his older sister, who is an academic superstar, and his parents felt ambivalent about singling him out, resulting in his not getting the help he needs. He is impulsive, angry, defiant, and, though he is not the mastermind, when other boys start making a list of girls (ranked in order of desirability), he doesn't want to stick out any more than he already does. These are all just reasonably well-informed suppositions, as I've been pushed out of the situation. Like Jonah, students like Julia would keep things from me—but I only realized this over time.

Sometimes, it's the kids who leave me out. Like Julia, Carmen, the daughter of Colombian immigrants who attends a girls' school as one of two scholarship kids in her class, likes to guard her truths carefully. She is the master of lost papers, of work that the teacher reportedly never returned, of upcoming tests that she has never heard about, of missed appointments, of assignments that never get done, of books she has never read. She lives in a web of small lies, not sure of her next step, afraid of failing and perhaps wanting to do so at the same time. She fills her notebook with exquisite drawings that show she is not as distanced from reality as it seems. She has captured every wrinkle in her art teacher's face. She knows exactly what's what, and she chooses to distance herself as much as possible from the world in which she finds herself.

Lost papers are kids' way of starting over, of asking for a new beginning, of pretending that they've understood when they haven't. Cheating has acquired a new patina in New York City private schools, as teachers struggle to keep up with the tech-fueled stratagems of postmillennials. Sleight of hand can still play a role. Lily tells me about a girl who has extra-time accommodations, as she does, who uses the study-hall period to slip her math tests into her backpack instead of returning them to the proctor. The girl knows that the proctor is busy with a number of tests, and then the math teacher does not find the test in her proctoring folder and can't grade it. This happens several times over the course of the year, and only to this one student.

Most kids don't need to cheat in obvious ways, though. If they are in the middle of a test that they don't understand, they feign sickness and go to the nurse. And if they don't do so in the middle of the test, they complain to their parents that they were sick during the exam, and then the parents email the teacher and ask for a retest because their child wasn't feeling well. There are endless variations of this excuse, including "I forgot to take my ADHD medicine at lunch." It's hard to know what's real and what's not, and one is forced into either being a dupe (if one accepts the excuses) or a shrew (if one doesn't). Most teachers have given up fighting against the current a long time ago and simply provide the students with a retest. I'm not sure what will happen to these students in college or post-college, where they won't be able to feign illness as easily and get away with it.

When parents are confronted with these incidents, they usually choose the most convenient explanation—one in which their kid was sick or misplaced the test. The parents' seamlessness, their constant staying on message, actually earns my admiration at times. I've known few who break down in the midst of a conference about their child's fail-ing grades or problematic behavior and claim, "You know, you're right. Our son should leave this school." Instead, most parents remain steadfast and usually find a teacher to deflect their anger on or find some proximate cause of their child's failures that hides a larger truth. For example, they'll say, "If only Mr. Samuels hadn't been absent the week before the paper was due" about a paper the child was supposed to be working on for an entire semester.

It's hard to find another private school if students have to leave their school—and this is part of the parents' resis-tance to leaving. To enter another independent school re-quires their child to take the ISEE or SSAT, which are very difficult tests that require months of preparation if taken seriously, and there are very few open spots in New York City. If a student has to leave in the middle of the year, there usually are no open spots, unless he or she is plan-ning on attending a special-education or other type of spe-cialized school.

There is also considerable loss of face for a student and their family if they have to leave a private school. It's not like leaving a public school, in which there could be some sense of shame, but not usually a loss of status. When a child at-tends a private school, parents often choose to focus at least some of their social life on the other parents at the school. There is morning drop-off every day, as well as afternoon pickup, not to mention the parties that are held outside of school. It can be very good for business to get to know other parents at the school, as they are generally well-positioned and wealthy. Having your kid leave the school can mean severing this social connection, one that might have been in place for years.

But lying can make this situation more, rather than less, likely to happen. Very early in the year at one of the schools I work at, a handful of kids start having problems that the admissions committee was not told about. These problems are even apparent on the camping trip that kicks off the school year, and they suddenly worsen in the early fall. One boy can't get out of bed, and he starts not coming to school at all. The admissions committee learns that this behavior started in the spring of last year at the student's old school, but they were never told—not by the old school or the parents. The school kicks into high gear, trying to get the boy the psychological help he needs after a whole summer when he received no help, but it's too little, too late. He tries to return to school and finds he can't. After that, I lose track of him. Another boy seems to be off to a promising start until the school realizes that he is almost incapable of speaking to adults. He has other problems at home, long-standing in nature, and he is sent off to a therapeutic boarding program during the first semester of the year. The parents had not mentioned anything to the admissions committee about their children's issues before admission, and the result is that their children are quickly in and out of the school, looking for a more therapeutic setting.

I understand the parents' desire to try mainstream schools and hope that their children's anxiety or other issues will dissipate as the year progresses. It's natural to think, "It's just nerves, and he'll do well once the school year starts."

My son has had to leave many schools that weren't a good fit for him, so I know it's hard to predict everything that will happen.

Still, there is a level of deception and misinformation that serves no one, least of all the kids. A girl at one of the schools where I work becomes so thin that her cheeks, once full, develop hollows, and her body is wizened. She develops that lollipop look favored by celebrities on the red carpet. Her parents mention nothing as the year drags on and their daughter looks paler and paler and her hoodies hang off her body. Not until the school nurse calls home do the parents and the nurse figure out that the student is taking extra Ritalin to starve off the pounds. Ritalin is the commonly prescribed amphetamine that effectively and safely treats ADHD—but that also was once used as a dieting tool in the *Valley of the Dolls* era. The school nurse requires the student to see her doctor and join a therapeutic group so that she regains weight and stops abusing her medication.

There is a great deal of obfuscation in these types of situations. It's not always clear how much the parents realize—or want to realize. Both boys and girls on Park Avenue tend to be very thin, as do their parents. There are few fat people in this social class. At the tony NYC private schools, there are about five kids out of five hundred who could even be called overweight. It takes me a while to figure out the stories behind the seemingly healthy bodies of my students. Most likely, these kids begin on a regimen intended to help them lose weight, such as working out with a personal trainer, and it becomes an obsession. Some begin running and not eating. They are lauded by others, most likely also their parents and possibly their coaches (though, to be sure, many coaches want kids at a healthy weight), and what starts out with healthy aims quickly spirals into maintaining a very low weight at which the kids are putting themselves at risk. Researchers believe that this type of calorie restriction can wreak havoc with the neurotransmitter systems in the brain.

Athletes are at increased peril of restricting their calories in ways that can put their entire eating into a disordered state. Many sports require kids to reveal their bodies in ways that some might consider intrusive. The girls on the volleyball teams in New York City private schools, for example, generally wear spandex bottoms that look like underwear. It's unclear whether an athletic advantage is conferred from high-cut shorts, but there is no doubt that the kids I work with, both girls and boys, who play these types of sports or who run competitively feel intense pressure, mostly self-imposed, to trim down. Many, such as Lily, still enjoy their food with relish, but others show the kind of restricted eating that can get people into trouble. What begins as a way to trim one's thighs under one's revealing volleyball shorts can snowball into binge eating.

If you've never seen binge eating, stop by the student lounge at most high schools around midmorning, and you'll get a firsthand look at it. It involves teenagers who routinely don't eat or sleep enough pouring sugar-packed and carbohydrate-dense foods down their throats in quantities that seem indigestible to most human innards. Sour Patch Kids, gummy bears, doughnuts, oversize bagels, and endless streams of lollipops: these are the foods that are consumed by binge eaters in a way that experts believe stimulates the deprived centers of the brain much in the same way drugs do. What results is a self-reinforcing cycle of dieting and stuffing oneself with foods that contain little more than sugar and guar gum. The starved brain is an addled brain. One that needs to be satiated with two bags of Swedish Fish before it temporarily calms down and then begs its owner for more.

Bingeing often happens in secret, which explains the corn chip bags, discarded Tootsie Roll wrappers, and drained coffees that regularly greet me on the desks and floors of my students at tutoring sessions. Bingeing is concealed, often, in tall Starbucks cups with the familiar green mermaid on the sides. One doesn't necessarily look gluttonous when consuming a Frappuccino, but the Venti Caramel Frappuccino delivers up 81 grams of sugar—just what a starved brain is jonesing for. And following that coffee, the teenage body of the drinker will be deprived of regular nutrients and subjected to grueling workouts, often from school sports and travel-team competitions, sometimes on the same day. Still, if the kids look trim and muscular, as many of them do, parents don't tend to consider kids who are unhealthily thin or who subsist on coffee drinks problematic.

The kids' bodies reveal a deeper story that's harder to decipher. Some high-school athletes get into a spiral where they are constantly breaking bones. Excessive exercise, such as what comes from participating on a school team and a travel team outside of school, combined with chronic injuries, should make parents and schools wary of what's going on for a kid, but often, these injuries are taken as a matter of course.

Walk down any New York City private-school hallway, and you will see a parade of crutches and casts. The kids are brave about toting them around, and some have even become expert at maneuvering with them. There are nicely set up buddy systems so that pals drag each other's backpacks around, and the metallic clang of crutches on the floor is a constant in the halls. Children of course are prone to injury as they throw themselves exuberantly around on the playground and sports field, and this is to be expected. But when one is as battered bodily as these children are when they play one sport with great intensity, it reflects a certain willingness to subject kids to the kinds of injuries that professional athletes face.

Kids' bodies are imprinted with the results of relentlessness and brutality, and the 1 percent of New York are seemingly more—rather than less—likely to endure these types of injuries. Most kids are subscribed to sports at a very young age, and they are encouraged to become experts in one sport. The 1 percent are not the only cohort playing sports so professionally and doggedly as children, but it does have the resources for additional travel teams, coaches, 5:00 a.m. squash practices, and trainers.

Concussions are all too common. They occur with such regularity, the result of sports played with intense competition and physical contact, that there are postconcussion policies that involve accommodations at most private schools in New York City. Though the medical advice on such things goes back and forth, it is generally advised that following a concussion, kids not look at screens for some period of time, until their headaches go away. Some kids stretch this out, claiming to get headaches weeks or even months after their injuries, to get the school to continue to go light on homework, even as the kids go heavy on Instagram and video games (in other words, they are, seemingly, just fine).

There is nothing dishonest about these injuries—or is there? There is a level of sports competition at which parents are not being honest about the results of the play on their children. How about the time these sports take? Sports are a beautiful thing, and no one could deny that. To have your child be part of something bigger, to help them become more disciplined, to feel the power of their body— all beyond beautiful and often much more meaningful than academics to most kids. Standing before a school football field, I can feel the sense of order and beauty that comes from forty kids all pulling together and running drills to get better at a collective effort. But there is a point, perhaps difficult to calibrate, at which parents and coaches, mostly of travel teams, move into a world of dishonesty because it has more to do with them than with the kids.

One cannot help but think of Jordan Baker, Nick Carraway's love interest in *The Great Gatsby*. Nick writes of her "slender golden arm" and her unflinching need for power that could only be soothed by victories on the golf course, even if they were obtained through deception. Jordan is a cold character, a woman moved only to win and whose competitive spirit allows her to block out everything else. And, yet, her participation in sports leads her not to Olympic heights but down to the depths of cool dishonesty. Kids trained to win above all else run the risk of growing up to be Jordan Bakers, not Michael Jordans.

★ ★ ★

It has long been conventional wisdom in our society that all kinds of crime are associated with the lower class, who, perhaps out of necessity, cheat to live. However, Paul Piff, a psychologist at the University of California at Irvine, and his colleagues stationed researchers at a four-way intersection in the San Francisco area and found that drivers of upper-crusty cars, identified by their age, appearance, and make, tended to cut off other cars and pedestrians more than drivers of less ritzy vehicles. In other words, the Land Rovers steamed ahead, while the Kias stopped. Now, it's possible that some rich people, emulating Warren Buffett, drive Kias, but these findings have been replicated in other studies these researchers have conducted. For example, adult subjects who had more money were found to take more candy from a collection that they were told was going to a group of children, as opposed to subjects with less money. People from lower socioeconomic classes, in contrast, were proven more likely to be generous, motivated by a sense of compassion and egalitarian values.

Piff and his colleagues believe that people from lower socioeconomic classes are more sensitive to those in their environment and that they tend to use helpful, altruistic behavior as a way to deal with their relatively deprived status. For people with fewer resources, it can be a very good coping strategy to help others because they might need help, too.

These results by no means signify that all rich people are evil and that poor people are noble. That is far too simple (though, the studies do make me think of a private-school father, stressed because his son was in trouble, shoving the dean's candy in his mouth—candy that was intended for the students). However, these studies suggest that those who have higher socioeconomic status expect to get away with more. That doesn't mean that people are inherently good or bad but that expectations travel with them in their social classes. This conclusion cannot be shocking to anyone watching the news, including the collapse of people with power who stoop to financial, sexual, and other crimes, over the past half century or so.

This tendency among the rich to believe they can get away with more shows up in the way I am paid. I am sometimes not paid. Rich clients are far more likely to take more time to pay me, or not pay me at all, than poorer clients. The parents for whom tutoring is a sacrifice (though I offer a sliding scale for these parents) pay me right away. The check is in my hand before I have to remind them at the end of the month or send them an invoice. The parents who can easily afford tutoring often tell me that they forgot to mail their checks. Some, even after the advent of PayPal, tell me that they don't know how to use these electronic-payment systems and haven't time to investigate. One parent routinely pays me months late but leaves his investment reports out on his kitchen table. Without meaning to look, I notice that he has about a thousand times my invoice in only one fund that was, the pie slice next to it showed, nicely invested in high-growth stocks.

In an effort to get paid, I've unraveled a few parents' lives that are built on layer upon layer of fraud. This is certainly not routine; most of the kids I tutor come from families whose parents want them to do well and who have every intention of paying me in a timely way. Once every few years, though, I engage with a parent who is a master of deception. One mother whose son's college essays I helped edit disappeared when I asked for payment. Once prone to emailing or texting me on a daily basis, she slipped the surly bonds of Earth and became unresponsive to emails, calls, and texts, even from other parents who knew her.

Her life proved to be a shadowy presence. Though she included a LinkedIn page on her email, there was no other presence of her decorating business online. There was little reference to her online, save for a Google site on which she had extended the reviewing function intended for restaurants and stores to everything, including her congressman. She had given her Botox-injection service high marks, but she was quick to dole out low marks for her luxury Manhattan apartment building, which had not, according to her badly punctuated review, readied her apartment promptly enough for her. Her only virtual fingerprint was the series of rapid-fire reviews. Her business addresses turned out to be virtual offices run by a Russian company, her résumé proved absent of any real companies she had ever worked for, and her name was untraceable. A cipher in the real world, she was a solid presence on Google Docs, which informed me that she had accepted hundreds of the suggestions I had made to her son's essays. As I received these virtual fingerprints of her using my work without payment, she escaped into the cosmos, unfindable, untraceable, and unaccountable.

And then there are the lost jobs. Though most of my tutoring situations work out, some don't. One family, whose son I adore, is in the midst of chaos resulting from a re-marriage. The stepfather resents the time he has to put in to his wife's son, who formerly attended a public school in Brooklyn and is now, after his mother's remarriage, attending an expensive private school on the Upper East Side of Manhattan. The parents have a professional chef at home, and they make it clear that with the entertaining they do for their jobs in the music business, they don't want me tutoring the boy at home. I meet him twice a week at school, and he makes some progress, but he still has lost papers that don't get handed in even after he completes them. He leaves them in the printer or loses them in the depths of his backpack.

The dad emails me to fire me. In all caps, he writes, "YOU WERE SUPPOSED TO HELP HIM HAND IN WORK. YOU DIDN'T. YOU ARE FIRED." I have tried to tell him that I can't ensure that his stepson will print his papers, as the printer is at home, and I can't get to their home. However, it is May, and weary from the academic year, I just let it go. I'm surprised when the stepdad pays me in full for the sessions I had with his stepson. Some years later, I see him standing outside a midtown office building smoking. He doesn't look up from the pavement. I always wonder what happened to his stepson.

I am fired by an Upper West Side mother after her daughter thoroughly prepares for a science test and then fails it. She uses multiple ways to learn the material and definitely knows it, but when she enters the test room, it leaves her head like a bird in flight. I am perplexed and unnerved by her daughter's constant failures when she seems to be so well prepared, and nothing in her neuropsychological evaluation explains why this eighth grader should lose hold of material that she has overlearned. I'm hoping that her mother will see this as another clue that can help us put together the puzzle, but the learning specialist at the school, who has met with the family already, informs me, "They didn't have very nice things to say about you," so I'm not surprised when they let me go.

When I press the learning specialist for what she really thinks is going on, she says she's not sure, but she thinks there is a chance that the girl is questioning her sexuality and that her propensity to choke on tests arises from a psychological fear more than a learning issue. I never find out what is really going on for this girl, or whether she gets over her tendency to panic. Her home is, perhaps, not the type that would have welcomed her experimenting with alternative sexual expressions or identities. Her parents have the airbrushed looks of pleasant Midwesterners who have moved to New York City and done very well for themselves. They are both tall, blue-eyed, and muscular, and their daughters are, too. The older daughter is a perfect student, and both girls wear outfits that involve bows in their hair and buckles on their patent shoes. The tutee's face is cherubic and round, and she put her heart into studying, into learning Latin, into memorizing historical material. She and her sister become overexcited about packing for a vacation to Nantucket, for which they and their nanny (who often stays over to watch them when their parents are traveling for business) slip pastel gingham clothing into Vera Bradley bags.

Their lives remind me very much of a stage set of *Father Knows Best,* though father is not often there, and I'm not sure how much he knows about his daughters. The mother seems more on top of things, smarter, more tuned-in, and very competent. It pains me that she doesn't like me or trust me. The more I try to explain that something else might be interfering with her daughter's learning, the more irate she becomes at me. I feel tongue-tied trying to explain a situation in psychological terms that I know wouldn't make sense to the mother, and she becomes angrier and angrier at what she feels are excuses. When I finally explain that her daughter might be anxious, and anxiety might be preventing her from learning, the mother rejects my explanation. "My daughter seems pretty happy to me," she says, and shortly afterward, I am history.

At the time, the experience stings, but what bothers me most all these years later is not knowing how the student makes it through high school and college with that level of hidden anxiety. It's true that she doesn't look anxious. As I get to know hundreds of students, I realize that not all of them wear their anxiety like they are Fielding Mellish in the Woody Allen movie *Bananas*. They don't all have bitten-down nails or stutter or try to find the answers to life in the *I Ching* like a textbook-neurotic character. Nonetheless, their anxiety is very real. It can be subtle, filtered through their adolescent ways of being and trying to appear chill. Their anxiety can be all-encompassing yet hidden to those around them, and it can take up all their mental resources so that there are none left to process the information they need to learn.

Early in my tutoring practice, I am fired by a woman who thinks I've done her son's fourth-grade math homework wrong. The problem in question involves calculating the number of pencils each child in her son's class would receive out of a box of twenty-five. I use the number her son gave me to work with him on the problem, but the mother has a different number in her head. She has simply forgotten how many students are in her son's class. In a way, we are both right, as what's important is the process, not the answer. She calls me when I've just emerged from the shower, and I explain how I did the problem after she interrogates me. She fires me, and many years later, I teach her son at a private school and discover that he has a subtle but debilitating writing disorder. Neither of us mentions the earlier incident, and the student and I work together on his writing until it improves. Even though she always paid me, the mother sends me a check for $350 many years later for no reason, and I believe that the lesson of that early pencil problem was not lost on either of us. We realize that we were both too quick to bristle and that her son was worth being really patient about.

The thing about these lost papers is that they are not lost. They are more like clues that help me as a learning specialist slowly put together what is going on for each kid. Lost papers are almost always recovered in some way, later on.

This is not meant to be an indictment of those with more. As I have written, I'm a privileged person, too, privileged with education and with the advantages I was raised with, but there is no doubt that most privileged people carry with them certain expectations about the way the world should function. They expect to get more and are often enraged

when they don't. These expectations can go largely unexamined. In the old days, they were almost entirely unex-
plored. It's hard work to acknowledge them, but we must
if we hope to live any kind of moral or enlarging life—the
kind of life that makes not only us better but the world
better, too.

The unexamined life means that we will continue to expect that we will be given things because we are wealthy
or privileged. Everyone has the right to hope for a good
life and to work hard for it, but not to expect it without
hard work. When I work with the parents of Park Avenue,
I find that they expect their children to get things without
necessarily working or that they expect that because their
kids work hard, they will automatically be given things. I
speak to one mother whose daughter has been thrown into a
deep depression after college admissions were sent out. This
girl is quite wonderful—a feminist, one who cares about
things and who is very gifted at science. She is upset because
she got into Johns Hopkins but was hoping for something
more. "She worked so hard, that's the thing," her mother
explains. Let's set aside the idea that Johns Hopkins is an
amazing university. Her mother's expectations, and those of
the student, are that hard work means that one will always
get what one wants. If only that were true, but it's become
something that many of the parents I work with have expressed along the lines of the following comments:

"He works so hard at writing, and he received a B−."

"I don't think you understand how hard she works."

"But she was up all night doing the assignment, and the
teacher still didn't like it."

The problem with these types of formulations is that they always couple hard work with results (the question of whether the students are really working that hard is a more perplexing one). It's comforting to tell children, "Just work hard, and you'll do well." I expect that for many of the parents I work with, they have worked hard and have done well, so they make this assumption that hard work and results can always go together for their children. No longer is the hard work its own reward. This is especially problematic for kids who have learning issues, as they may work hard and not receive results. Julia was a student who had to work twice as hard to get a B−, and she often dipped into C range in her AP course. Lily is continually exhausted just trying to keep up, and I have to tell her "Yes, you will work twice as hard and may not get the same results as everyone else." She seethes at the girls in her school who seem to get As effortlessly.

Still, there is something to hard work, to knowing that one has labored hard and long on something. It means taking the work away from those who evaluate it. It's like the boat one crafts from birchbark that looks rough-hewn and even ugly but that is the fruit of one's own premorning labor when no one is around. It's the best one can do, and the desire to do labor for its own sake is what sustains effort over time. But the affluent make a transactional connection between hard work and the payoff. Maybe this is true of many kids, but the rich expect the payoff to be more sensational.

Lost papers are truly lost opportunities. Students would rather claim a loss than fumble and be wrong—or just admit fallibility or laziness. Their inclination is to deflect their issues onto something else, and a lost paper becomes a convenient target. It is instead a reflection of everything that bothers them or makes them feel insecure and that they refuse to grapple with.

The lost papers accumulate in my mind over the years that I work with New York City kids, almost as if they are mounting up like actual piles of papers. They become symbols like the golf ball that the character Jordan Baker is supposed to have moved in *The Great Gatsby*. There is a rumor that Jordan cheated, though it was never confirmed, much like the lost papers I have encountered—or, more precisely, not encountered. Nick Carraway thinks of the vapor of rumors that surrounds Jordan once he has been around her for a while and gets to know her. But he doesn't entirely blame her for being dishonest, "incurably dishonest" as he calls it, because he sees it as a defense against the harsh world that surrounds her.

The missing tests, the lost term papers, the missed meetings with teachers, are like Jordan's misplaced golf balls. They enable kids to survive in a harsh world, one in which they feel that they can't otherwise survive. Like Jordan's golf tournament, their worlds have high stakes. If they are going to rise to the level of competition, they have to practice sleight of hand, to become masters of the carefully misplaced paper.

7

Stolen Moments

In a childhood filled with lost papers, moments of joy and abandon must also sometimes be stolen out of time. The moments when kids truly experience a release come without warning, in the midst of studying for AP tests, taking the ACT, having private squash lessons, and FaceTiming their friends. These are not scheduled moments but flickers of light that break through the clouds.

The kids I tutor and teach don't really know how to have fun, unless it's lubricated with alcohol. During the end of senior year, after their college applications have been electronically signed and sealed on a system called Naviance that tells them exactly what their chances are of getting into each college on their lists, they dissolve into a kind of Jeff Spicoli–inspired torpor that is more defiant than relaxed. They radiate to the world that they can't be bothered to do school anymore once their college applications—the reason for doing school in the first place—have been submitted. Their actions are entirely cynical. They transmit, as they arrive late to class and don't do their work, as students who once fought for Bs slide joyously down to Cs, that they've played the game, and now, burned-out, they can't be bothered to tune in. School is entirely transactional—a chance for admission to a prestigious college—and not much more, save a chance for socializing.

In their feigned insouciance, these seniors are playacting, simply copying what they have seen in B-grade teen movies. To them, relaxation involves wearing flip-flops, being out of dress code, and sleeping late most days. They are either coerced into playing the game of school or slide into complete and dramatic sloth.

Every once in a while, I see them in Csikszentmihalyi's state of flow, so at one with an activity that time passes unnoticed. It's the opposite of the way many students I work with live most of their lives, pushed from one thing to another, avoiding, evading, and stomachaching their way through tasks. I often wonder how they look when they're on the squash court or soccer field, because their participation in the rest of life can only be described as halting, half-hearted, and erratic. They participate in travel teams but often only crack a smile when practice is canceled or when they talk their parents out of making them go. "I am not going to squash today!" Lily cries with glee on a hectic Monday. "That way, I can get to bed before eleven."

Trevor is better able than most kids to shake off the mantle placed on his thin shoulders and to be buoyant. He is completely relaxed with younger children. He has the playful attitude and no-nonsense demeanor to break through to the troublemakers who would annoy adults. While working at a soccer camp with younger boys, around nine or ten years old, he gets them to wash their hands by saying, "When you're older, you're going to like girls, and girls don't like boys with dirty hands." They queue up to the sink and wash their grubby mitts wordlessly, probably in as much confusion as awe. Trevor is a pied piper, a line of small children following him wherever he goes, chanting his name at soccer games, wanting to be like him when they grow up. At home, he hums as he totes furniture around the basement, and he gets his clothes dirty. He sits on the wall outside and eats a sandwich with the maintenance guys, his laugh carrying into the courtyard.

Lily has an eye for fashion, and she has covered her walls with details from *Elle, Vanity Fair*, and *Vogue*. She neatly snips pictures of interestingly made-up models (think: canary yellow eyeshadow that actually works, models on the catwalk wearing wraparound skirts and thigh-high boots). Since she has to wear a girls' school uniform with a plaid skirt, she can only wear these fashions on the weekends.

Preparing for the Gold and Silver Ball, a black-tie charity affair to which students at elite NYC private schools (and New England boarding schools) are invited, Lily's in a state of ecstasy. It's not because of her date, who is a family friend, but the fact that she finally has an audience for her willingness to experiment with fashion—a style that she can't display on most days of the year. She sports a silver shift and metallic purse. Somehow, all the sheen looks great on her, as she sweeps her hair into a messy bun and tops it off with a velvet cape. Her statement is in the way it comes together as she models her dress for me and her mother.

Though it's regressive to say, in some ways, she would have been better suited to an earlier age, when women wore elbow-length black gloves and were not expected to excel on the squash court and in the classroom. She cannot explore this side of herself, though, except on rare occasions like the ball. Lisa, her mother, joins in the festivities, taking pictures as Lily sucks in her cheeks and poses the way she has seen models pose in *Vogue*. She and her mother are excited together, finally working in tandem, to prepare for the event.

"Mom, can Campbell come over to take pictures?" she asks.

"Right now? It's a school night, and you have Blythe," Lisa says.

"Please! Just for a few minutes, so we can post to Instagram? Please?"

When her mom is still distracted with her phone, Lily goes over and places her hands on her mother's and shakes them up and down until her mother looks up. "We have to get more people to go to the ball, and they'll only go if we show them our dresses. And what if we wear the same thing—disaster!"

Her mother nods and agrees. Lisa puts down her phone, or at least cradles it without looking at it, while watching Lily and her friends Campbell and later Liv rock their dresses and shoes and makeup and post their photos on Instagram and Snapchat so that their friends will be enticed to come to the ball. Lisa laughs as Lily tugs down her shoulder straps and twirls around, and she says, winking at her daughter, "You're hot!" and mimes having burned her hand.

After the ball, Lily's walls are plastered with photos of her posing in catwalk strides with her friends, fully in her element. Those photos stare back at her as she resumes her daily grind of squash lessons, tutoring, and test-taking. They are frozen forever in time and begin to fade and peel off the wall as the sunlight enters her room. There are no fresh photos to replace them.

Sophie, who is a swimmer, delights when she has a foot injury and cast that prevent her from taking part in practice. I've come across this phenomenon many times—kids who don't chafe against a bodily injury but who welcome it because it means that they can stay on the sidelines for a few weeks and get some rest. One student I worked with at a very demanding Manhattan private school confided in me, "Dr. Grossberg, don't tell anyone, but I hope the basketball team loses so we can stop having practice every day." He spoke in a whisper and looked relieved when I told him his secret was safe with me. When the team kept winning and advancing in the playoffs, he became more and more exhausted and dispirited. There was practice six days a week, only Sundays off, and the coach often made the players run until they vomited. Members of the student's track team ran every day—sun, rain, snow—often in shorts. I wondered if a tornado would stop them.

Sophie, with her large shoulders and long reach, is a good

swimmer, but she wants nothing more than to be out of the pool for a few weeks. Her mother draws attention to Sophie's weight gain in a teasing way one day before tutoring, pinching Sophie's slender middle and telling her to "lay off the chips." I can't see any evidence that Sophie has gained an ounce, but I can tell that she looks a lot better rested and happier. Kids praying for injury so that they can get a break—a break for a break—is something I thought I would never see.

Fun is something that sometimes has to be pushed on kids. Washed in the glow of video screens, they have seldom been exposed to the simpler pleasures. When I, along with other teachers, take a group of private-school ninth graders to the woods in the Appalachians, many of the kids are just plain freaked. Though we are glamping in cabins with clean wooden floors, workable window screens, and flushing toilets, the kids are too amped up to sleep. Many have never really left the city—at least not to go out in the woods—and the proximity of the chirping birds unnerves them. When the skies let loose and there is a nice round of early-fall thunder, a wave of vomiting ensues. One girl seems to be really sick—and she heads off to the nurse's cabin (deluxe in comparison with ours)—and the others seem simply homesick. When I was a toddler, I had already been camping in a slumping canvas tent alongside bears that mauled our trash, but these kids have never been this close to nature at night. In one three-day period, they have to endure thunderstorms, homesick crying jags (keep in mind they are fourteen), and busing their own tables.

During free time, when they are allowed to shoot hoops or go canoeing, they seem as joyous and energetic as you'd expect kids to be until one them—whose bones are thin and have been made brittle by playing one sport for too long—breaks her wrist making a layup during a pickup basketball game. When we return to New York City on a Friday afternoon, the kids sigh with relief, and their parents are waiting in their SUVs to take them to the Hamptons where, it is apparent, they don't interact that closely with nature.

I have never understood why the children of the affluent—at least, some of them—are not allowed to chart their own course through life. Why are they not allowed free time? Their own choice of career? Why is every moment guarded? Many of them will have the freedom—and money—to choose, in theory, any path they want, but they are instead steered toward a limited roster of choices. In these kids' lives, every moment is transactional, leading to money-making careers or, in the case of many of the women, to money-making careers that lead to marrying people who will have money-making careers. When Trevor takes the PSAT, he has to pick his intended college major so that colleges can potentially recruit him. He scans down the list of careers, looking for real estate, and I laugh, thinking he's joking. Later, I realize that his parents have told him that he will enter real estate—not as a lowly broker as I had thought he was joking about—but as a major player in commercial real estate. His conception of college is so transactional that I have failed to understand it.

This transactional nature governs a great deal of what the

affluent do, including having fun. Gatsby himself saw entertainment as a means to an end: his house was to attract parties, his parties were to attract Daisy, and even his shirts were to impress her. But all his transactions were aimed at earning love. At the end of his property, he could see across the bay to the green light at the end of Daisy's pier. His parties were to find something like love, as he conceived of it with Daisy.

It's not always clear what the 1 percent are looking for. It is clear that, from a young age, they have constructed a schedule for themselves like Gatsby did in the flyleaf of a *Hopalong Cassidy* book. Gatsby, then James Gatz, developed a self-improving schedule that involved fifteen minutes of barbells and wall-scaling each day, followed by an hour of studying electricity and two hours of studying "needed inventions." He allotted only half an hour for baseball and sports, as if to contain his fun. The reader is left wondering how much Gatsby adhered to these self-improving exercises, as he later made his fortune through connections to gangsters and a possible involvement in throwing the 1919 World Series. Gatsby's route to riches was not eased by hard work and self-improvement as much as by graft, but he was raised in the American religion of adherence to strict times and to the ethic of self-betterment against all odds.

Trevor's family, and others like his, worship also at these twin temples, though they are set up in direct opposition to each other. Like the young and impressionable James Gatz, he is held to a tight schedule and relentless self-improvement through rigorous schools, workouts, sports games, and tutoring. His parents also know, however, that they must at

times resort to greasing the wheels of his future with donations—which is not graft but which runs counter in many
ways to the ethos of self-betterment. Still, they are bireli-
gious, observing at both places of worship.

Among the kids I tutor, Warren, son of the multigenera-
tionally rich, seems to have the best sense of how to shape
his free time. He is able to practice instruments and play
music many days a week, and he decides to learn foreign
languages just for fun. I often find his parents with an open
copy of the *New Yorker*, and they continue to ask him about
his writing. He rarely looks tired and stressed, and he often
sings under his breath as he opens the door to me for our
tutoring sessions. I love stepping into his house for an hour.
He offers to make me tea, and he is so thoughtful about
what he writes. Over the course of our work together, he
develops strategies that help him emerge as a very gifted
writer. He has the stuff—deep attention to detail, a knack
for a pithy, witty phrase, the capacity for analysis—that
makes his writing not just clear but beautiful. And best of
all, it is not torture to him. He loves reading and writing
and thinking, and he takes the time to do so.

Born into a family that was established even around the
time of the Civil War, Warren is the closest figure to the
Buchanans in *The Great Gatsby* (though, unlike Daisy and
Tom Buchanan, he and his family are kind). Some of the
family relics hang on the walls of his house, such as portraits
of bluestocking women. I am not from this class, myself;
instead, like most of the students I work with, I am from
the Gatsbys, the strivers, the creators of the new American

dream. My people were turn-of-the-century Russian and Polish Jewish immigrants to Jamaica Plain, Massachusetts, where they worked in shoe factories, and to the Bronx, where they worked sewing shower curtains, and to the Lower East Side of Manhattan, where they made alcohol in the bathtub during Prohibition.

Does one have to be from Warren's people to feel that the world is lovely, as he does? His parents aren't obsessed with money, and they have passed this along to him. Every time I pass his brick loft building in SoHo, decked in a wreath for Christmas and flower boxes in the spring, it seems to offer the promise of what the light at the end of Daisy's pier promised Gatsby—the ease, the comfort, the style of knowing that you've arrived.

Unlike the Buchanans, Gatsby did not really know how to have fun. The Buchanans' fun often ended in disaster and disruption, but they were avid about playing polo and golf and taking joyrides. For Gatsby, on the other hand, each moment was considered, each party dedicated to an end goal rather than a reckless abandonment of cares. Perhaps the American religion of capitalism as a whole forbids this type of hedonism. Whatever the case, it is foreign to most of the children I work with.

They, too, have gotten used to parceling out time for dedicated aims. When they are left to their own devices, they generally don't know what to do with unmarked time unless it involves losing themselves to alcohol or drugs or video games. Even pursuits that seem hedonistic aren't really. One of the students I work with becomes a professional race-car driver at the age of sixteen. He leaves New York to travel to races around the country. Racing involves training each day on simulators, thinking about turns, working out with a trainer, thinking about one's next race. He has the burdens of a pro athlete even before he's gotten his license. The only place where it's legal for him to drive is on the track.

On one glorious May day, in order to free up classrooms for AP exams for juniors and seniors, Trevor's class is allowed to go to Coney Island with some teachers. The students have never been. They approach the subway nervously, as most have not taken it as far as Brooklyn—far, far into Brooklyn, where they will decamp at the end of the line. Along the way, the subway emerges above ground at points, and they see parts of New York most of them have never been to. They spend the journey shooting spitballs at each other out of plastic straws.

Let loose on the raunchy, rundown boardwalks that were thronged in Gatsby's time, they gaze at the ocean. "Is that a house of prostitution?" one student wonders aloud, looking at the ramshackle, boarded-up houses along the boardwalk. I wonder if he's ever heard the word *whorehouse*. This possibility clearly interests him, and he is more animated than he is in class. The kids eat at Nathan's for the first time, enjoying french fries as the sand whips around them. They try in vain to frighten seagulls away from swooping down on the fries that have landed on the ground. They get badly sunburned and almost get lost on the subway home. As soon as they return to the Upper East and Upper West Sides, they head to squash, running, and baseball practice. One day stolen out of time. The next day, they'll be back at school.

8

The New College Try

Most of the world has now heard of the college-admission scandal that sent wealthy parents to jail for hiring people to take tests for their children, bribing college athletic coaches, and faking their children's sports participation. While these shenanigans were extreme, they exposed both the desperation that many privileged parents feel when their children apply to college and the consultancies that will help them along the way. After all, the college-admissions process is the drawn-out Super Bowl of high-stakes parenting. There is winning and losing and nothing in between. Remember Deflategate? When the Patriots allegedly deflated the balls of the opponent for an advantage? (This is still hotly debated in Boston.) Well, Park Avenue parents make attempts to deflate balls, so to speak, when it comes to getting their kids into college. There is endless strategy and conniving. And the outcome—which college a kid gets into—is a referendum on the entire season, meaning their entire upbringing. Few fans say, "Well, at least we got to the AFC Championship Game this year." Similarly, few Park Avenue parents say, "Well, thank goodness we got into Kenyon." No, winners in the proverbial game of college admissions go to the Ivy League or Stanford, for the most part. A few other colleges are passable—the University of Chicago for eggheads, maybe Williams and Amherst. For those who want to save face because they can't get into an Ivy: Oxford in the UK. Off the list: colleges no one has heard of, experimental colleges, and "anything worse than Middlebury" (which is a prestigious liberal-arts college in Vermont). Part of the problem, as the parents see it, is that schools like Yale will only take a few students from each private school, and they try to get a geographically diverse class, so the students would be better off applying from public school—or a state like Mississippi that doesn't generate a lot of Ivy League applicants.

So, let's just make the rules of the game clear before we start analyzing the entire long season that leads to the Super Bowl. To their parents, every kid is Tom Brady. Every kid is destined for greatness, if only they can find the right team. If a kid isn't heading for Yale, it's because the team isn't right. I will try not to be too tiresome with this Super Bowl metaphor, but it really is apt. Assembling the team starts early. Some parents—many—start after eighth grade. In Sophie's case, her support staff was already assembled long before I met her.

"She's working with some people in Westchester," her

mother informs me during Sophie's ninth-grade year. "They just want to vet you to make sure you're a good fit."

That means that I have to speak to the college-consultant team, none of whom seem to know anything about learning differences, and explain my work with Sophie. More specifically, I have to speak with a certain Noëlle, who sounds like she is all of twenty-three. While emailing her to set up a time to speak, it annoys me to no end that I have to include the two dots over the *e* in her name, but I know she will be peeved if I don't. The diacritical mark is part of her self-important presentation.

"We are trying to balance Sophie so she is stretching herself but is still successful," Noëlle explains to me. The boss, the head of the college consultancy who has written a book on getting into college and who worked for a short time at an Ivy League admissions office, is too busy to speak. I wonder what she is doing. Trying to talk Hillary Clinton into writing an applicant's letter of recommendation to Yale?

"We are trying to help Sophie really *reach*," she says, stretching out the word so I get its meaning, "but of course, we want her to be happy," Noëlle continues. "She's just a bubbly, happy kid."

I'm not sure whom she is speaking about. The Sophie I know, the girl of empty Limoges boxes, is not a happy camper. She's malleable, and she plays the game really well. But she's not happy. After the shoplifting incident, her parents buy her a pair of diamonds just like the ones she tried to steal. They seem to think that she was searching for the perfect earrings.

"I hope Sophie is happy, too," I mutter back, at a complete loss. I hate that I cannot think of any better response.

Sure that I am going to be fired by the college consultancy and considering adding two dots to my name (Blÿthe? Blythë?), I'm surprised when Sophie's mom tells me that the consultants loved me. "I mean, *loved*," she explains. "They think you're perfect for her." I suspect that my Harvard degree has a lot to do with their referendum. Still, I'm a bit tickled. It's not the kind of affirmation most children of the '70s hear every day.

The college consultancy decides that Sophie should sign up for some summer classes. The problem is that there is nothing she is truly interested in taking, but they search the catalog at Columbia and come up with some STEM-related and obscure history classes, and one in playwriting to make her seem well-rounded. Of course, she must be tutored through those classes, which is why I wind up tutoring her in Russian history during one long, hot summer. I'm familiar with the momentous events in Russian history—the freeing of the serfs, the killing of the czar, the pogroms that my grandmother spoke about as if they were yesterday. But this is Russia in the Middle Ages, during the time of Kievan Rus. It turns out that I love this stuff, and I spend a lot of time trying to explain to Sophie how fascinating the ancient Russian fear of the Mongols is. She spends most of the tutoring sessions looking at her split ends and then cramming her head full of facts for the final. She is so adept at cramming that I'm amazed. She can memorize an entire list of medieval Russian leaders. I simply feed her lines, and she knows them, cold. After she aces the final, I mention the famous Mongol invasion to her, and she responds, "Huh?" as if she has never heard of it. But she has the A from Columbia on her transcript.

Sophie's parents have been playing this game for as long as they can remember, and they are all experts at it. Ben's parents are far too late to the party. Convinced Ben needs more attention, and perhaps an evaluation to determine if he has any underlying learning differences, I try to reach his mother in vain. She answers my call, says she is eating dinner, and never calls back. I see her in the newspapers, at society events, but she doesn't return my calls or pay me. My invoice for $600, covering several weeks of tutoring, remains unpaid far into the summer, as I read about her family at golf tournaments on Long Island.

Though she is rarely involved in her son's schoolwork, his mother becomes intense about his college-admissions process once Ben starts senior year, regarding her son's education as another tournament. She snaps into focus, making demands of the school admissions counselor and Ben's teachers. The problem is that he's been struggling up to this point. Described in kinder terms as a *mama bear* by Ben's school administrators and in less flattering terms by his teachers, his mother insists that the school support his application to colleges like Princeton even though he doesn't have the grades or scores for admission. Having lost a great deal of their fortune to ongoing lawsuits, the family can't pave their son's way with a large donation, and he slips into a large Southern college, where he is barely noticed. His mother returns her attention to her golf game.

The problem that most kids run into is not their sports bona fides, as they've been coached since they were tots, or even their grades, as they've been tutored every step of the way. It's standardized tests like the ACT or SAT. I don't think these are good tests, and as it turns out, they predict far less of a student's chance at college success than do grades. After all, a student sits down and takes a test a few times, while grades in high school are a measure of a student's performance over time. A student who doesn't know the formula for finding the area of a trapezoid but who has the persistence to meet with her professor and go to extra study sessions is going to do better in college than the apparent genius who can get a perfect score on the SAT math section but who never gets out of bed to go to class.

Researchers have confirmed my hunches. Herman Aguinis (then of Indiana University's Kelley School of Business) and his colleagues found, using samples of hundreds of thousands of students of different racial backgrounds, that the SAT does not accurately predict grades in college. For some groups, the SAT overpredicted their performance, while for others, their scores underpredicted it. The results of looking at over 475,000 students showed that these tests are not reliable measures across different universities, colleges, or subgroups of students.

Aguinis's study is a thorough mathematical debunking of the myth of the validity of standardized testing that I long ago stopped believing in. I have tutored kids who've gotten perfect or nearly perfect SAT or ACT scores who have actually failed out of college. One student in particular was a very sweet boy who aced the SAT math section without really trying. His speed at solving math problems was enviable and something I could never hope to emulate. He understood them intuitively, while I plodded through alge-braic formulas that I'd learned in tenth grade. I was work-ing with this student on his executive-function skills—the ability to plan, organize, and manage his time, among other skills—while he took a break from college, and he admitted that his math skills had done him no good. "I mostly used them for online gambling," he cheerfully admitted. He had a lovable sense of his own failings, and he ultimately decided to spend some time at a community college improving his study skills before deciding what to do next.

It's true that there is that kind of student who scores fairly well on the SAT because they have read a lot but who also is devoted to learning. I was one. But SAT or ACT scores must always be considered as only one part of the larger ap-plication. It seems odd to me that students spend many hours and thousands of dollars preparing for these tests when their grades are mediocre. A student who applies with high scores on standardized tests and low grades will be branded with a giant U (or a similar mark) for *undermotivated*. I am surprised when parents of mediocre but smart students plow a bun-dle of money into upping their kids' SAT scores when high scores are the worst thing this kid can present to a college. Perhaps the parents reason something along the lines of "At least he'll show the colleges how smart he is!" but colleges don't generally want underperformers. The parents would be better off saving their money for their child's music les-sons or other extracurriculars.

SAT and ACT scores in a vacuum are next to worth-less, but they are a barrier to entry for the schools that most of the kids on Park Avenue want to get into. While many colleges have made these scores optional, the Ivy League and equivalent schools still require them, mostly as a way to weed kids out. They have far more qualified applicants than they can admit, so the tests become one way to winnow down the multitudes. And while many of the students I work with have benefited from superlative teaching, they are not readers. They simply do not read on their own, and when they are faced with difficult reading passages on the SAT, they run aground. Though they have been spoon-fed reading in class, they have no real familiarity with dissecting difficult texts, filled with idioms, misdirections, and varied narrators. The questions on the test throw them. This section is difficult to tutor in. Students can easily bring up their math scores, but if they aren't readers, if they haven't spent years sitting with books on their own time, they generally can't outwit this section. Their high socioeconomic status means little if they haven't read.

When I was at Harvard as an undergraduate, I met other students who had never heard certain words outside of books. They knew words like *autodidact*, but only from having read them. If they heard a professor pronounce these words, their eyes spilled over with tears of joy, and they often mispronounced these words until well into their sophomore year because they had only seen them in writing, never heard them said out loud. In these cases, reading had trumped socioeconomic status. The kids on Fifth Avenue often have the opposite problem.

I have tutored dozens of kids in these tests, and I liken it to hoeing a massive garden filled with broken pots, weeds, and poison ivy. It is my job to clean up the gardens, create neat rows of flourishing plants. There are many kids who are facing reading passages from the nineteenth century or from Japanese literature who cannot master idioms or expressions. Their misuse of little words marks them as people who don't read, only as oral consumers of English. Their sense of what is grammatically correct comes from watching YouTube videos, and they become combative when I tell them that their favorite microinfluencer doesn't speak the Queen's English.

Looking over her ACT essay, I tell Sophie, "*Based off of a movie* is incorrect. The right phrase is *based on a movie.*"

"*Based off of* is, like, totally correct," she sighs, blowing air up to her bangs.

"It's correct for spoken English, not written English. There's a difference."

"Whatever. Why is the ACT so uptight?" she asks, flinging her pencil aside. I recognize her gesture as an act of frustration, not rudeness.

Later, when I ask her to analyze the sentence *Yellowed with age, my grandmother removed the dress from the box*, she is in a flippant mood, and she replies, "What's wrong with that? My grandmother *is* yellowed with age," but I know she has already learned to spot a misplaced modifier and she knows the sentence is grammatically wrong. Sophie is very quick, but the work we do on grammar, writing, and idioms during our sessions preparing for the ACT is only a game to her. It devolves to rules that she can follow, such as when you see a description, make sure it is followed by what it is describing. There is no need to get into a deeper explanation of misplaced modifiers. It means nothing to her, just another exercise in memorization, much like the way I mastered my Torah portion for my bat mitzvah. ACT tutoring is a rite of passage for her, just as the prom will be when she is a senior. She passes through it like she passes through everything else: wisecracking, but getting by. She has even finished, ahead of schedule, the community-service hours she was given by the judge for shoplifting. She showed up on time, forked up trash, and moved on. Nothing seems to touch her or faze her.

Sophie takes the ACT three times, and she sits through endless tutoring sessions. Her parents sign her up to take mock tests at a Manhattan testing center, and they monitor her progress. She is able to sit down and go through the test several times before she actually takes it, and her surroundings come as close as possible to replicating an actual test center—an advantage few kids across the country have.

She is about to tip into the 30s (the ACT is scored from 1 to 36, and more competitive schools require scores well into the 30s), which will give her a definite edge, along with her classes at Columbia (though she had long forgotten Kievan Rus) and the internship she completed, through her mother's connections, at a Madison Avenue art gallery. She can play the game, and she keeps working, mastering the tricks that I've given her for the English section and a smart Columbia grad has given her in math, and she earns a composite of 31. That score and the straight As she has bullied her teachers into giving her are good enough to get her into a Seven Sisters school, one of the prestigious East Coast women's colleges, where I think she will thrive. Sophie is very much like Cher in the movie *Clueless*. She doesn't really understand the larger picture of what she's doing, but she will do it until her teacher relents and gives her a high grade just to stop Sophie's complaining. She is all set to do very well in life.

That is—if she can think of something to write about for her Common App essay. This is the essay, with a maximum of 650 words, that every student must write as a part of the application used by most colleges (some also add short supplemental essays to their individual applications). It's a blank canvas, a chance to tell the colleges something that is not apparent about you from the other parts of your application. Kids are used to writing about Scout in *To Kill a Mockingbird* or about Daisy Buchanan in *The Great Gatsby*, but they are not used to writing about themselves. It's a daunting task, and the economy of words you must use is, if anything, an obstacle rather than a help.

For the parents, the problem with the Common App essay, which is an open-ended personal statement, is that experts like the officious Noëlle can't write it for the kids. They can, of course, but the admissions committees have a good nose for essays that don't sound authentic. It's like the essay that Lisa wrote for Lily on *Romeo and Juliet*. The work must be authentic. It must sound like it came from the kid. It must dovetail with what they have already written, or it will be a jarring element in the application, out of place. The idea has to come from the kid, but the topic also can't be something that is obvious or overrepresented in the rest of the application. Lily has spent her life playing squash every morning and afternoon, but she can't write about that for her essay. Instead, it must represent a world, a moment, an epiphany that the admissions committee doesn't know about yet. The obstacle is that these kids haven't been able to experience many moments of epiphany, as every minute has been scheduled for them. Epiphanies occur, as they did for me growing up in small-town Massachusetts, in the maple-ringed field where I was watching my neighbors' sheep (and, apparently, not realizing how to keep them from impregnating each other), or in the Shaker graveyard I wandered with its simple iron crosses marking the burial sites of 150 years ago. These kids haven't had time to wander; they haven't had moments in which inspiration has come unbidden to them.

Packaged moments do not make good college essays. No admissions committee wants to hear about a public-service trip to Costa Rica that the student's parents paid for. That's not telling them much. No one wants to hear about a student's summer frolics in a luxurious resort. No one wants to hear about a student's successes on the athletic field. What makes good fodder for the essay are random moments of insight, or humiliation, or truly entering some unknown world. College applicants from the 1 percent often mistake crossing geographical boundaries as crossing psychological boundaries. This can be true, at times. Travel can open minds, but it often doesn't because luxury trips insulate travelers from deeper discoveries, and even if it does, it's hard to capture the experience in words and be truly reflective.

I sit with a senior named Noah before his new MacBook Air, and we scroll endlessly through the question prompts for the Common Application essay. Noah can't think of anything to write about. I prompt him. I provide him with strategies to help jog his mind into thinking about those private moments in which he came to an important realization. We take out his childhood photo albums, and we pore over them, looking for people, events, anything that helped form him. At the end of this exercise, we are knee-deep in photos of baseball games, family dinners, school concerts, and vacations, but still nothing occurs to him.

I can't give him ideas. I can look at him from the outside and tell him what I think might set him apart—his mother is Japanese while his dad is French—but I still can't tell him why that should be interesting to him. If he begins to use my prompts, he will sound inauthentic, and that's the kiss of death for the Common App essay. After days and days of thinking, he decides to write about how his mother is Japanese and his dad is French. The essay never sings. It hums along for a while, but it never sings.

One of the best college essays I ever read was by a student named Khalil, whose father was involved in importing oil from the Middle East. This student rotated a collection of Rolexes on his wrists. Some were vintage, some were new, all were ultracostly. He looked like the kind of kid who would be arrogant, unbearable, and cocky, but he was, in actuality, humble, sweet, and kind. In part, his learning issues had humbled him. In a family filled with superachievers, he struggled academically. In his essay, he spoke about a physical collision between his research index cards and his teacher—actual physical contact—that resulted in his realization that he needed help. He was thankful to his teachers for bringing him along, and this humility was reflected in his essay. He wasn't afraid to write about how often he had failed, what he had learned, and his continued need for support. It seemed like a counterintuitive essay—it wasn't the typical admission of a small fault only to reveal a larger strength. The essay brought out his continual struggles, his lack of confidence at times, and his need to connect with his teachers and professors to feel more confident and do well. But it was exactly the kind of essay that admissions officers like because it had texture, realness to it. No one was writing this essay to please or impress others. Khalil knew himself as a student, and the admissions committees were impressed by his maturity.

Contrary to conventional wisdom, there is no slam-dunk method for writing college-application essays. There is no magic topic about which to write, no overarching lesson to leave your reader with. It's not an elevator pitch but more like a ten-minute conversation—the type you might have if your elevator stalled between floors for a few minutes. You might be scared, you might feel moved to tell your fellow captives something about yourself. You might tell a story or explain something about why you are hoping your elevator doesn't plunge ten stories to its depth. They would emerge knowing a bit about you. If you keep in mind that the essay is a longer, vulnerable conversation, you will understand why a male student I worked with, who was a star squash player, decided to write about his friend coming out of the closet. He didn't choose to write about squash, as the admissions committees already knew he played squash. Instead, he wrote a heartfelt essay about how his friend came out on a school camping trip and how the other students supported the friend. It wasn't flashy, but subtle. Each word was carefully polished. It had the shine of an underwater bank of stones, and it wowed the committees so that he was admitted to an Ivy League school and a highly competitive liberal-arts college.

Warren, the boy with the potter father and banker mother and generations of Harvardians, also writes an essay that is almost beautiful on its first pass. Warren is one of the rare kids who seems genuinely happy, in part because he enjoys the life of the mind and the world of music. He reads so much on his own, starting with myths when he was younger, that a book in his hands takes flight in his imagination. He has the internal cues, the words committed to memory, to make new readings resonate with him. He can pass them along through his memory and bounce them off the thousands of other readings in his brain. His punctuation and grammar are at first errant, but after two years of working with him on structuring his writing, I can confidently tell his parents that he no longer needs me. His college essay, which he asks me to look over, is, after just a few drafts, close to perfect. He writes about how much reading dystopian stories have meant to him, how they provided an escape to him as the youngest child in a family of strivers.

Warren is the type of student who would have floated into Harvard in earlier generations. He is an intellect who is an exquisite writer and who has, by junior year, become a superlative student. The problem is that during his ninth- and tenth-grade years, he was still working on his writing and study skills and had some lower grades, and admission to colleges like Harvard requires preternatural maturity. There are some schools that like to see an arc, a trajectory toward maturity, in a student's profile, but Harvard is not necessarily one of these schools. Although his family members have attended Harvard since 1900, although they have given millions in the past, although he is a genuine intellect, and although he earns a very high score on his SAT, although his essay shows real thoughtfulness, it may not be good enough for Harvard.

College consultancies that want to package applicants try to give them novel, cutesy techniques to write their college-admission essays. For example, they suggest writing about why you are like your favorite color of nail polish. But this type of trope only goes so far. The applicant has to make it real, and even a modicum of adult meddling can make the essay ring false. This is why, after brainstorming with a kid about what they want to write about, I step back and let them do the writing. The only thing I'll do is nip here and there and suggest different ways to structure their thoughts. If the essay is a sculpture, the marble is theirs, and all I do is help them cut it down to size. A student I knew submitted an essay about how much different books meant to him while he was a solid C student in English class. (Though it's possible for a dedicated reader to do poorly in class, this wasn't his case. He had rarely picked up a book for pleasure reading.) In writing the essay, the student's voice must be heard—and their parents can no longer run the show. Another student I worked with even wrote about his battle with irritable bowel syndrome and likened himself to a samurai. I thought it was ill-advised, but it was clever, and it certainly caught the admissions committees' attention. He was admitted to a top-flight Midwestern state university.

The best way I know how to tutor in the ACT or SAT is to make the kids learn the stuff. There are some tricks, sure, but I think that when the kids are wasting so much time studying for this test, they might as well master the math they never learned.

There are companies that charge $800 an hour for this type of tutoring. The cost is self-glorifying, as is the process. These companies tend to only employ tutors who went to Ivy League schools and their equivalents and received perfect scores on their SAT or ACT. Many of these tutors are trying to make it as musicians, writers, and actors, and they find they can make a good living by tutoring in these tests. The high cost of this type of tutoring, however, means that tutors must justify themselves. They have to earn results.

Many of these tutors are lovely people. What they are not is therapists. They don't always understand the way in which they are making their students go slowly insane. They are also academically gifted but not necessarily people who love to teach, and they don't tend to understand kids who learn differently than they do. Their methods, as far as I can tell, are to subject the kids to endless memorization, assign a lot of homework, and have the kids take full-length practice tests each weekend. They resemble nothing so much as drill sergeants.

Lily's mother explains to me that her daughter will receive tutoring from one such company, the Hermès of the tutoring world. They may not offer a different product than other people, but it's marketed as better, and it's certainly more expensive. It's constantly amazing to me that parents will pay these types of fees for SAT or ACT tutoring, and it's too facile to say that money means nothing to them. Instead, they believe that they are purchasing their children the best that money can buy. It's not clear that this is true even some of the time, but the tutors at these high-priced companies tend to get results because they are relentless. Most of their magic, as far as I can tell (and I'm sure they would have a different story), is that they subject the students to so many practice tests that they are almost on autopilot when they are taking the real SAT or ACT. The students have simply seen every type of question beforehand, so they know how to solve them. Of course, the tutors play a role in helping students figure out the questions and sort them into differ- ent types. I've known similar types of tutors who charge one-quarter of what these high-priced ones do.

The other problem is that high-priced SAT or ACT tu- tors see their work in a vacuum. They don't care that the kids are also contending with very difficult junior-year work (though, some offer tutoring in academic work as well). Something's got to give. Kids don't have enough time to dedicate themselves to top-level academic work and to endless rounds of SAT or ACT tutoring and to their sports and other extracurriculars. This is where I think the whole thing becomes self-defeating. There are some students who can pull it off, but for many, the SAT homework becomes too much.

Lily is this type of kid. She takes hours to do her home- work, and she is tutored around the clock. She spends the rest of the time shuttling back and forth to squash practice and games, and she travels to squash tournaments on the weekends. She is like the Cat in the Hat from Dr. Seuss, trying to juggle a dozen different things as she goes down the stairs. One more thing pushes her over the edge, and she becomes tearful when she is faced with SAT homework on top of her regular work.

The truth about the SAT or ACT is that you can do okay and still get a lot of questions wrong. I have worked with balanced kids who judge that a 27—out of 36—on the ACT is just fine for them in the math section, and that means that they can get 15 out of the 60 math questions wrong. But if you're on Fifth Avenue, your parents may want you to earn almost-perfect scores, which is impossible for most people to do. I went to Harvard and did not earn even close to perfect scores in math. My verbal scores were high because there was absolutely no pressure on me to perform. I remember going in to school on a Tuesday morning in the late '80s in the fall—one of those perfect autumn mornings in New England—and thinking that I was lucky that all the vocabulary on the PSAT (which used to feature an analogies section) used words I had heard of before. I was the kind of dorky, bored kid who read Jane Austen and asked my mother all the words I didn't know. I came up with a perfect score on the verbal section without any tutoring or prepping, and my guidance counselor was pretty happy with me. My parents didn't respond much when I told them my scores. They already knew I would do well, and they were more concerned about my staying healthy. When I went to take the SAT, held at Lawrence

Academy in Groton, Massachusetts, it was now a perfect summer morning, and I remember the communal concern on that May Saturday was the location of the party for later that night. Driving away from Lawrence Academy, I was happy the onetime rite of passage was over. That was the only thinking we dedicated to it. What was important at my public high school was having the right sunglasses as you left the SAT—not what your score was.

Lily's life is oriented differently. Her ACT prep starts well before her sophomore year, so she has two years of prepping before taking the test. Her mother has mounted a six-month campaign to get her daughter extra-time accommodations on the ACT. The problem is that Lily suffers from anxiety rather than having a definitive diagnosis of a learning issue. Students who have documented learning differences can take the ACT or SAT at their schools if they have certain accommodations, other than just 50 percent extra time. These include multiple-day testing and using a computer to write the essay. The ACT in particular grants these accommodations to kids who really need them, meaning that the student has proof of testing, conducted by a neuropsychologist, showing that they work slowly or have attentional or other issues that mean that they benefit from extra time and other accommodations. To think that all kids who use accommodations are gaming the system is not to understand the true nature of learning disabilities. There are people who process information more slowly, and giving them extra time is a way to level the playing field. I've been informed by skeptics such as Trevor's father that "There is no extra time in life," but most situations in life, unlike the SAT or ACT, are not timed. The imposition of time limits is artificial in any case, as it's not like real mathematicians or novelists usually work with a time limit. The tests themselves are flawed, as is the very conception that a timed test can get at real knowledge, and accommodations are necessary for certain students.

Often, if a student has a clearly defined learning issue that has been well-documented, they are granted these accommodations. However, students like Lily work slowly because their minds are strained by anxiety but don't have a definitive diagnosis. The ACT is reluctant to give students like this accommodations, and they reject Lily's first request for extra time and the opportunity to take the test over multiple days. Lily's mother resubmits the request, and the ACT rejects that, too. What follows is an expensive round of retesting with a Manhattan neuropsychologist who charges $8,000 out of pocket for a thorough evaluation to document learning issues. He teeters on the edge of making an ADHD diagnosis and decides that there is enough evidence to do so. With this new diagnosis in hand, Lisa applies for Lily's accommodations for the third time, and they are granted. At this point, Lisa's assistant is handling these requests. It requires several hours of her time to make sure the school has all the paperwork it needs. It has taken six months, endless reams of paper, and an $8,000 evaluation to get Lily the ability to have 50 percent extra time and to test over several days.

Lily is relieved, and it's easy to see that she can benefit from these accommodations. She is anxious and works slowly but methodically. But her situation raises larger issues of equity. If students can afford these expensive types of in-depth evaluations, they are more likely to receive accommodations, as evaluators know how to write their reports so that they will pass muster with the College Board and ACT (though in recent years, the College Board generally allows any student who has received extra-time accommodations at their schools for a certain number of months to receive these same accommodations on their tests). Parents like Lisa have endless resources to make sure their children receive accommodations. Lisa has two assistants at her bank, and one of them works assiduously on this project as if it is as important as putting together one of Lisa's megadeals.

Most parents could not have carried out this fight. For one thing, many parents rely on their school districts to have their children evaluated, and these evaluations tend to be skeletal and formulaic. They don't look deeply at a student, for the most part, and they don't give students much attention. In some parts of the country, such as New York City, it is almost impossible to even get a Board of Ed evaluation, as there is a long backlog. If a student gets one, it usually just comprises an IQ test and some academic testing, and it lacks the full battery of tests that private evaluators use, such as tests of memory, language, attention, executive functions (the ability to plan, shift tasks, prioritize, and carry out other functions related to organization), and psychological testing. Therefore, evaluations conducted by public schools are likely to miss a lot of what private evaluators get.

Lisa also has the womanpower of two assistants to help with Lily's request to the ACT, and the college-counseling and learning-specialist staff at Lily's school help her at each step of the way. In many public schools, there is simply no one to submit requests to the College Board or ACT, or, if there is, they are too overwhelmed with work to submit these requests. In contrast, the staff at Lily's school works over the summer to submit requests, and they still scramble on the day before the deadline to submit all the needed documentation to the ACT. One of the learning specialists at Lily's school even pulled her car over on an upstate New York thruway and used the internet services at a local diner to make sure that Lily's papers were submitted on time. This is the kind of service that parents at private schools often receive. A poor student at a public school would likely not be evaluated or, even if they were, there would not be staff to submit their request for accommodations to the College Board or ACT. There certainly wouldn't be the kind of staff that submitted these requests multiple times, as Lily's school did. Single parents, parents with two or more jobs, parents without assistants could not have waged this fight.

Lily's intent is not to cheat, but her mother wants to make the testing as favorable to her daughter as possible. She consults with Lily's psychiatrist about when would be the best time of day for Lily to take each section of the test, and she asks the proctor, who is an employee of Lily's school, to cater to these hours.

"The proctor said she couldn't do 12 noon, which is really Lily's best time, according to the doctor," she explains to me. "I said we could get our own proctor, but apparently that's not allowed."

"Your own proctor?" I ask incredulously.

"Yeah, I mean, if the proctor couldn't make that time, I could find another proctor. But the school said that for this type of testing, the proctor has to be someone employed by the school."

"That makes sense," I say, stammering. "I mean, you can't just hire your own proctor."

"That's what the school said. So I put in a call to the head of the Upper School so they could find another proctor for Lily."

I imagined the person in the college-counseling office who was trying to arrange Lily's test was not keen on the idea that Lily's mother had intervened to find a proctor for her daughter's testing when she was trying to work it out on her own.

"I know it's the day before President's Day break, but I'm hoping the head will get back to me."

I have definitely entered the hall of fun-house mirrors that becomes Lily's ACT experience. The school eventually finds an employee who can proctor each of Lily's subtests at 12 noon over several Saturdays, but Lily isn't looking too good on the eve of her test. She meets with her ACT tutor (I'm not tutoring her for the ACT) for several multihour sessions the week before the test, though I'm not sure what advantage that can give her at the last minute. She reports that the English subtest, which tests grammar, went well, but when she goes in for the second day for the math test, the situation begins to unravel.

She is unsettled by the ticking of the clock in the room where she is taking the test, alone with the proctor, and she mentions this to her mother when she gets home from the test. When she is crying to her mother, perhaps trying to protect herself from the blame of receiving a poor math score, she also drops into the conversation the fact that the proctor miscalculated one of the times by a minute. This sets off a firestorm of protest. Lisa fires off an email, hastily worded and angry, to the proctor, the head of the Upper School, and the head of the college-counseling office, demanding that the ACT be informed of these "glaring irregularities," as Lisa calls them, and petitioning the school to tell the ACT that Lily deserves to be retested without waiting for the next official test-administration window. The head of the college-counseling office manages to talk Lisa down off the ledge, and the ACT is not informed of the loudly ticking clock or the apparent minute that Lily might have lost.

In the week leading up to the weekend when Lily will take the reading and science sections of the test, she looks beyond peaked. Her face is pale, and she chews her fingernails down to the nubs and insists on watching Harry Potter movies from her youth. When she returns from the test, she is devastated. In a call that her mother makes to me, she explains, "Lily had a panic attack during the reading section. I'm not sure what happened, but I'm here with her. I canceled my trip to Buenos Aires." It's ironic that the woman who missed Lily's eighth-grade graduation to travel for work has canceled a business trip for Lily's ACT debacle. Lily's father, a quiet man who works in publishing, is also hanging with Lily at home, it seems. "Do you think we can call the ACT and ask for a retake?" Lisa wants to know. I explain that Lily can just wait until the next test administration. When I hang up, I can't believe that Lily, a passionate reader who appreciates *Paradise Lost* perhaps more than any other nonacademic, has had a panic attack during the reading section of the ACT. I fear that reading has been forever tainted for her.

"I felt like the room was closing in on me, and I couldn't breathe," she explains later, as she circles her neck with her hands to pantomime what it was like for her. "I mean, I couldn't read, and the words just kept bouncing before my eyes. I filled in the bubbles, but it was, like, totally random. I am sure I failed." She laughs nervously, aware that there is no such thing as failing the ACT.

When her scores come back, they aren't half-bad. She has scored in the upper twenties in most of the sections, and even a respectable 25 in reading, and her composite, or overall score, is a solid 26.

Her mother looks at Lily's score report and says simply, "I'll ask the doctor for a beta-blocker for the next test."

Trevor's parents are far more practical. They have more money than Lily's family, and they decide to use it to their advantage. Trevor has the same high-octane SAT tutors that Lily has, but he doesn't do the homework, and though he has extra time on the test because of his diagnosis of ADHD and dyslexia, he generally finishes the test early. His scores are disappointing, and though he receives a second round of tutoring, his scores on the second round are only slightly higher. The Earl of Grantham and his slim, disdainful wife receive the score reports without comment. They are composed through each step of the process.

I then hear through the SAT tutor working with Trevor that he was accepted into the same Ivy League school his father attended. "The Earl of Grantham just made a bee-line to the development office," the tutor tells me. "He kept writing checks, and the development office kept looking at them and saying 'Bigger, more zeros.' Finally, they got to a place where they could all be happy, and Trevor was in."

I am at first outraged by this. But then, I figure, it does only one person harm—Trevor. In fact, the earl's check will likely pay for several scholarships for needy students. The earl has only hurt his son by telling him that he can't achieve anything unless it's paid for. Trevor doesn't have good grades or scores, but I know that he has dreams of doing something different from his father. He once told me that he learned everything from his father. Before I can figure out how to respond, he explains, "I just do the opposite." Though Trevor's parents expect him to follow the family path into banking or real estate, he has different plans. He tells me that he would like to marry early, which is interesting. After a string of girlfriends, he has settled into a cozy, supportive relationship with a student at an Upper East Side girls' school who reminds me of the Duchess of Cambridge, minus the tiara. He is very affectionate toward her, and I think he hopes to be a more loving father and spouse than the Earl of Grantham has been. He also wants to go out west, he says, and spend a few years "just hiking around and maybe doing some fly-fishing." He has a large marlin that his grandfather caught mounted on his wall, and this inspires him.

If only Trevor could be allowed to go west, to be free

of expectations for a while, but he will now be heading to the Ivy League, courtesy of his dad's large check filled with zeros. The kids at Trevor's high school are contemptuous of him, though they mostly keep it to themselves. Other students I tutor snicker at him and retell the story of his father's donation, which gets larger with each retelling until it's impossible to know what amount was really given.

However, the students are more openly critical of the college admissions of the students of color who attend their schools through programs such as Prep for Prep. These programs have helped students of color attend private day and boarding schools for decades, and they have provided a way in which students without privileges in New York City can get access to a top-flight education. They have to be selected into these programs based on testing and teacher recommendations, and the students I teach (and tutor pro bono) from these programs are incredibly bright. They also offer a different perspective than that of most of the kids, as their parents tend to work as nurses, public-school teachers, and New York City bus drivers. Many of the students are African American or Latinx or come from Africa, Asia, and the Middle East, and their parents sometimes don't speak English. Working with these parents tends to be very different from working with the Fifth Avenue parents, as they don't necessarily feel that they belong at the school and are wary of making waves.

Luke, one of the students I work with at a private school, is from West Africa. When he is caught smoking pot in the school bathroom—as many students are—it is a far different equation for his parents than for the privileged parents who come in with their lawyering-up antennae bristling at such moments. Though they may be privately mortified by their children's behavior, they are litigious and combative toward the school. Luke's parents, Ghanaian immigrants, have a different mindset. They first apologize to the school and make him apologize. There are no veiled threats, only the fear that their son could lose his scholarship. If a privileged student gets in trouble, there are safety nets—therapy, an evaluation to determine if he has learning differences, possibly another private school. A scholarship kid who gets in trouble is in a far more precarious position. Luke is able to continue at the school, and the school pays for his substance-abuse treatment, but every time I see his mother until graduation, her jaw is set squarely as if in anticipation that her son might not have the life she had dreamed of. Only at graduation does she stop clenching it.

Students of color at private schools are few in number, even in diverse New York City, and they offer the kind of perspective that other students often don't. When those students get into college, white students seem to think it is a result entirely of some fictitious preferment from affirmative action. Even parents at private schools are fairly uniform on this point, as competition to get into the Ivy League from the top private schools is intense. The parents and students know that only a certain number of students will be taken from each school. It doesn't matter that many of the students chosen are legacies—those whose parents went to the school—and those who can make very large contributions to the development office or who know people like senators or university presidents who can pull strings for them. Or that other students are recruited to play sports. But these types of admits do not generally garner the type of criticism that the admission of students of color do, even though they are clearly more than capable of doing the work. This supposed affirmative action is a topic that enrages white students. I've heard feedback from them many times. Once, during the heated week of Ivy League admissions, a gaggle of white students gathered in my office, where one of them said, "Of course Luke got into Yale. The Prep for Prep kids always get in." They might have substituted *Prep for Prep* with the name of their private school, as these students had a very high rate of admission to Yale as well, but of course they left that out. Internalizing prejudice from some of their parents, the media, and society at large, they developed the idea that Luke was somehow not qualified to go to Yale, though their reasoning was vague. It seemed to boil down to the idea that many white students were more qualified than Luke, though who or why was left unsaid. They were bitter on the subject, and when I reminded them that several students had gotten into prestigious colleges in part because their parents had gone there, they maintained that the legacies were qualified to get in. These students have not moved beyond the long-standing arguments that attempt to discredit the programs that broaden access to elite universities.

The "Middlebury problem" is very real to these types of students. A student who does not get into a top school feels somehow lesser, and the standards are unrealistic and extreme. There are a few free thinkers who head off to Whitman College in Walla Walla, Washington, or to Indiana

University at Bloomington (both very good schools), but for the most part, students are vying for spots at a few competitive schools. At some high schools, that means the Ivy League, Stanford, and perhaps MIT and the University of Chicago. At others, it means top liberal-arts colleges such as Williams, Amherst, Swarthmore, and the like. In reality, Middlebury is just as good as any of these schools, and it's a distinction without a difference. At each private school, there are conventions of what is a good school and what isn't.

Where students go to school is more than just a summation of their grades and scores. For many parents, it seems to be a referendum on their parenting. It is only natural for parents to want their kids to get into a good school, but this goes beyond any sense of helping their children receive a good education. They want control over a process that is not entirely within their control.

When these parents lose ownership of the process, they feel disbelief. The college-admissions process is one of these moments. Even when faced with the hard data from Naviance, the parents will be incredulous if they are told their child is not likely to be admitted to their school of choice. For most of their adult lives, these parents have been told yes. When they are told no, they become more primitive in functioning. They mount personal attacks on the college counselor, they bad-mouth other students in the class whom they think have a better chance at admissions, and they even try to malign these higher performers with school administrators. At times, I am at the receiving end of this ire, when students don't earn the grades their parents think they are capable of. It's at moments such as these that I glimpse the anger that underlies their superachieving personas.

In an era without God, college admission conveys sanctification on believers. The religion in these circles is achievement, and acceptance to a prestigious college means one is favored by the heavens. It's not entirely clear why getting into a specific school is so important, as attending Yale really achieves the same results as attending, say, Middlebury. But there is some belief that attending a school like Yale will give students the surefire route to future wealth and perhaps happiness, which flies entirely in the face of reason. In this religion, names and brands are like holy words. The parents must also justify the exorbitant sums they had spent on private-school tuition, sports training, travel teams, tutoring, test prep, and other expenses.

I have seen parents become irate on this issue. One mother, whose son received a B+ in a math course, called the school, bubbling over with rage. "We have sacrificed for years to send our son to your school," she told the head of the Upper School. "And it wasn't to get Bs! It was to get into the Ivy League." The chain of reasoning doesn't make sense until you realize that many of the parents have been sacrificing to send their kids to schools that cost over $50,000. Some parents can pay the tuition without blinking an eye, but, for others, it requires a huge strain, and they do so because they think it will improve their child's chances at college admissions. It's still not clear to me whether one B will wreck a kid's chances to get into a top school. It *is* true that overall, students from private schools have many advantages in college admissions, but there are bright kids who can also distinguish themselves at public high schools. In addition, there may be less competition at public schools to get into these types of colleges. It is not always a safe calculus to assume that a child who goes to private school will earn admission to a prestigious college. Instead, they will likely receive more teacher attention, read a greater number of books each year, write more papers, and be exposed to more cultural influences and possibly travel opportunities. They will speak—or at least know—the language of the elite, and they will be able to use it. This is what a private-school education does for most kids, and it is entirely worthwhile with or without an Ivy League admission.

But when parents and students are nearing the finish line and they see graduation within sight, many of them entirely take leave of their senses. Alex's parents suggest to him that he work with me to write a book on some subject (it's not clear what). He is plenty bright enough to write his own book one day, but he doesn't have time to write it alone now, given his upcoming tennis tournaments. "I would put my name on it," he explains. "But we would pay you for the writing."

I'm half-inclined to take it, thinking of my son's upcoming summer-camp expenses, but then I feel ashamed of myself and disgusted at the prospect. "I can help you write it, but you have to write it," I tell him. It never gets written.

In reality, Alex does not need any kind of help. In some strange way, he is a genius. He is befuddled, without friends, and becomes addicted to smoking pot. Ironically, it isn't another student but one of his tennis coaches that introduces it to him—while his parents think Alex's time training is entirely on the up-and-up, it isn't. He quickly becomes addicted and steals from his parents' petty-cash pile to pay for it. His parents often keep several thousands of dollars in cash stashed in their desk, so this proves easy for him. In spite of it all, he gets into an Ivy League school, early decision. His tennis has helped, but he has almost-perfect scores on the ACT and straight As. He is effortlessly Ivy League material. No money exchanged hands to get him in, though it's clear that his parents are in a good position to give money to the school down the road.

Alex has won the race, if it can be considered that, but it's not really clear what the spoils will be. He will attend an Ivy League college, and then what? How will he get to his job in the morning? How will he make conversation with his coworkers? How will he ever find a significant other? These are questions I can't figure out for him, and his college can't give him the answers, either. I'm not even sure how he will be able to get to his dorm room, since his parents' driver takes him everywhere.

For every kid like Alex and Sophie who has managed to grab the brass ring, there are several more who seem to fall short in their parents' eyes and in their own eyes. It's particularly crushing for children from the families who have built up long legacies at schools like Harvard and Yale. Nate was that kid, the one whose father, grandfather, and great-grandfather had all gone to Princeton. He was expected to keep up the tradition, and he probably would have, thirty years ago. He was the kind of kid who is smart, but A−smart, not A+ smart. He wasn't good at math, and the stress of that told on him. To get into Princeton, even as a leg-

acy, he would need straight As and a high national ranking in swimming.

He was humming along until junior year, when he wound
up in the class of a math teacher who had a hard time com-
municating with his students. This man had taught at some
of the most prestigious New England boarding schools,
and he was flummoxed by students who didn't understand
math as he did, as a language that he spoke fluently. Nate
wound up failing several tests, and his face became strained
and pale. He was convinced his teacher didn't like him because he had turned religious and was going to church each
Sunday, while his teacher was an atheist.

"The teachers don't understand God in this place," he
liked to say. Nate applied early action to Princeton, meaning that he applied in the first round, which includes a
smaller pool of generally wealthy students. Applicants who
need financial aid do not generally apply during early action (which is nonbinding, while early decision is binding,
meaning that an admitted student must attend that college),
as they want to compare financial-aid offers from different schools. Wealthy applicants have an advantage in applying early action or decision, and kids like Nate try to
work this advantage. Still, Princeton wait-listed him, passing him to the general pool of applicants, and rejected him
in that round. It's common for schools like Harvard, Yale,
and Princeton to give a student like Nate a "courtesy waitlist," which means that they don't reject him outright but
place him so low on the waitlist that he has no chance of
getting in. However, Princeton rejected him, ending the

multigeneration legacy for his family. He was crushed. His parents were angry.

He relived the C+ in math, the swim meets where he was slow, the moments when he was all-too-human and Princeton had found him wanting. All his achievements, the history paper he had earned an A on, the swim meets he had won, the way he now thought about becoming an army chaplain were lost to him. He only thought of the missed opportunities, the seconds he might have shaved off his swim times. He went on to Johns Hopkins, which he and his parents considered a second-rate school, and while studying theology, began to develop drinking problems. He kept looking for God but not really finding him. The last I heard he had taken some time off and was getting sober.

Warren is at first wait-listed at Harvard when he applies for early admission, the first round of admissions. That means that he is tossed into the pile of general applicants. Of course, he is not exactly tossed, as his status as a legacy will mean he is looked at more favorably. He goes through the rest of his senior year, continuing to revel in his reading. He is not fixated on going to Harvard, and neither are his parents. He has applied to a number of other good schools, and I sense that he will be happy wherever he goes. The *New Yorker* continues to be open on his kitchen table, and he continues to read appreciatively what his teachers put in front of him. His parents' main questions to me have always been "Is Warren writing better? Is he taking the time to revise his work?" They are concentrated first and foremost on his skills. In May, he writes me a thoughtful email to tell me he's gotten into Harvard and to thank me for my help.

And then there's Lily, my Virgil, my guide to the under-world. She knows the circles of hell well, having dwelled in them at her all-girls' school. She knows the hell of relentless bullying, of having to take the ACT with a beta-blocker and still falling short, of having to play squash at dawn. Despite all of her coaching, her squash rankings keep falling. I check on them on the internet because I don't want to stress her out by asking her directly, watching as she slips well below 100 nationally.

On the night when most of the college-admissions no-tices arrive, I am with her, working on one of her final high-school papers. She is writing on Anna Karenina on the day that colleges email their news—so-called Ivy Day. The Ivy League sends students to portals where they can see their admission status. Lily has been trying to get onto the portals for hours, and they keep crashing because so many people are trying to access them at the same time. While I wonder if she can return to Anna Karenina, she wordlessly goes on Facebook, where classmates are posting news about their own admissions. The news of who got in where has already gone viral. She finally gets onto some of the sites and finds out that she has compiled a string of rejections.

It's pointless to try to direct Lily back to the novel. She cannot feel the travails of Anna Karenina, rejected by her lover, without her child, and tossed out from society. Like any teen, she is concentrated on her own inner turmoil, and as she reads about Anna's death, she registers no emo-tion. Though she could easily relate to the devils in *Paradise Lost*, she is now beyond the reaches of literature, caught in the recesses of her own mind. She is thinking about how she will be able to get through the next several days, with her classmates brandishing their acceptance letters and their college sweatshirts.

Lisa, who has defended her daughter throughout middle and high school, now rushes to Lily's defense, treating the colleges who rejected her like the mean girls who once tormented her daughter. "Those Ivies don't know what they're missing," she tells Lily. "The admissions people are just wowed by the glittery gals and guys. My girl is solid, and they just can't see it." She believes that Lily's talents include being more conscientious than other people and less willing to compromise her values. She is correct in this assessment, and Lily's teachers wrote glowing recommendations of her as a person and student, so these qualities were reflected in the admissions process. However, Lily would not necessarily be happy at a large, competitive, impersonal college. She needs a campus where she can forge relationships with her professors and meet with them outside of class, and where she can go to a writing center to get help revising her papers. In Lily's case, the college-admissions process has placed her at a college where she is poised to be happy and flourish.

Though Lisa's message to her daughter may be flawed, it serves the purpose of uniting Lisa and Lily, who band together and feel exuberant that Lily is accepted into a solid, small school with a reputation for being the place kids attend when they can't get into an Ivy. Lily returns from her visiting weekend elated, and she explains that "I met a girl from Connecticut. When I saw her monogram necklace, right away I knew we were going to be besties!" Before she leaves for college, she throws her expensive squash rackets into the incinerator of her building. She plans to spend her free time sewing.

9

Citizenship

On a brilliant early September day, ten juniors from a New York City private school and I, their teacher, walk a few blocks in Brooklyn to a community organization. Clad in tight jeans, shorts, and tank tops, they carry Starbucks cups, as they are still unused to the early hours of school after the long summer vacation.

When they settle in at the cramped tables in the organization's main room, the director, a young man with a lot of hair product, tells them that they will be helping immigrants from all over the world to pass their citizenship test. He quickly passes out packs of cards with questions and answers, and the kids begin to quiz themselves.

"How many members in the House of Representatives?" asks Maddy, a blond girl wearing a revealing tank top.

"Two hundred?" ventures Sam, a boy who looks younger than his age.

"Four hundred and thirty-five!" says Calvin, an African American boy who greets the first person to arrive, a woman from Guatemala.

As the morning goes on, the students each develop their own style of teaching. Some are quiet and respectful, while others become ebullient cheerleaders. They surprise me by trying to coax a woman who wants to give up by telling her "You're doing well! Keep going!" Rachel, who claims that she doesn't know any Spanish and wants to drop the class although she has traveled in Mexico and studied the language for many years, speaks with a beautiful accent in Spanish to a couple from Honduras. Sam, who ranks at the bottom of his class and who never does his work, is the star of the show. He has a group huddled around him as he helps them figure out ways to remember the information and explains terms such as *impeach*.

"Dr. Grossberg, I think I could be a teacher," he tells me with a broad grin. It's the first and only time I've seen him excited about anything.

I am so proud of my group that I take numerous photos of them (which is allowed by the school) and send them to the dean who coordinated the event. The happiness of that day floats me through several weeks of applying for students to have accommodations on the SAT and ACT— byzantine processes that are heavy on paperwork and low on personal satisfaction.

The morning on which the students work with the immigrants at the community organization is their brief shining moment. After that one day, they return to the grind of school. Sam never completes his work. Rachel continues to doubt her ability in Spanish. They all look routinely tired and only want to play electronic trivia games when they're not in class.

These students have gained more emotionally from going to the immigration center and working with the immigrants there than the immigrants have gained in knowledge from working with the students. Private schools, recognizing the value of public service, have made service a requirement for graduation, but students often wait until the last possible moment to get their service hours finished, and they often choose activities such as walking in fundraisers. This type of service is worthwhile, but it doesn't give students the same perspective as working with people in need.

Many private schools seal their doors to the public. The way they try to effect social change is by providing scholarships to girls like Carmen, who attends a private school through an educational access program that readies her for accelerated academic work. But Carmen often feels displaced at her school, as if she doesn't belong, coming from Queens. There are at most one or two students of color in her classes, and her concerns—cultural, economic, psychological—are not often mirrored by her classmates. It's hard for her when the typical return-to-school conversation might go like this:

CARMEN: So, what was the high point of your summer?

TYPICAL STUDENT: We went to our beach house for most of the summer, and that was great.

Substitute *country house* or *ski chalet* at different times of the year, and you get an idea of how Carmen might feel left out.

Students of color and students who are from different socioeconomic groups have reported to me and others that they don't feel that their parents are welcome at the school. Sometimes, their parents don't speak English. Often, their parents work, some at multiple jobs, and cannot take off in the middle of the day for parent-teacher conferences. I taught one student whose father, who was from the Dominican Republic, worked in asbestos removal and could never leave work in the middle of the day without losing pay. He could never attend a parent-teacher conference, except by phone on his rare days off. Private schools accept a few students from other kinds of backgrounds but don't open their schools fully to them.

Could New York City private schools open their doors to the community in ways that would enrich them and their students? It's worthwhile for students to travel to other parts of the city, a world unto itself and one with which they are largely unfamiliar. I once brought a group of private-school kids up to a public school in the East 120s, and many had never taken the subway at all. Few had taken it that far north in Manhattan. Getting off at Lexington and 125th Street, they were completely turned around, unable to get to 128th Street and Third, until I reminded them that the street grid is similar uptown to the Upper East Side. They had never realized this basic fact about their city—that Lexington and Third and the other avenues travel north beyond their neighborhoods. Kids need to leave the confines of their private schools and travel the city, but the city also needs to come to their schools.

There are different ways this could happen. The New York City private schools could open themselves up to giving classes to kids from different backgrounds, or kids who don't go to private school could come by the school to benefit from the help of its teachers or college counselors. For example, college counselors at top private schools could provide workshops or counseling sessions for students at public schools that have only one guidance counselor for hundreds of kids. It's true that teachers and college counselors are already strapped for time, but the school can make provisions for them to have space in their schedules for this type of pro bono work, much as law firms do. Students themselves could also be involved in tutoring kids from other schools.

This type of exchange has the potential to benefit kids on both ends of the socioeconomic ladder, and it is these types of kids who make up a lot of New York's population. The middle class has been squeezed out, and those who remain tend to be from the very poor and the very rich. The kids in these groups have more in common than it may at first appear. They often struggle with anxiety, depression, substance abuse, acts of criminality, and missing parents. Of course, the rich also have resources to protect their children when they get in trouble, unlike the poor. Both groups need adults around them who value them for themselves and who take the time to know their individual wants and needs.

I have worked with both very poor and very rich kids, and their neediness has a similar quality to me. When I was a teenager, I worked as a counselor-in-training at a Y day camp near Fitchburg, Massachusetts, a declining mill town. Each day, taking the bus to camp, a seven-year-old boy named Clarence would board the bus and slide into the seat beside me. He would then latch onto me with his arms on mine and not let go until we reached camp. The other counselors and I called him the Spider because of his tenacious grasp and long, bony arms and legs. He never spoke. It was clear he needed reassurance from us.

He came to mind when I worked at an NYC private school where kids entered my office at all times of day, often just to sit and shoot the bull. They didn't say anything of importance, but they liked to sit and be in an adult's presence, an adult who would listen to them. I don't mean to be insensitive to the added pressures and inequalities of the poor, but I have noticed the similarities between the kids of the very rich and the very poor. Of course there are very well-loved rich kids and neglected middle-class kids, but the system of high-achieving schools that affluent children attend is designed at times to ignore them as emotive human beings and to emphasize achievement over what is desirable or even feasible.

Dismantling the athletic-and-academic industrial complex that has been built around affluent children might take a while. It's been reinforced by decades of shibboleths and false beliefs. Parents whose kids are barely out of toddlerhood brag about how good their kids are at soccer and speak about them getting college scholarships from their sport (which is very unlikely). When most kids are getting involved in travel teams at a young age, it's hard to be the lone parent who wants to reclaim family night and playtime. It's hard not to get involved in the excitement of wanting our kids to excel, and kids who don't play on travel teams don't have many options if they want to improve. After all, if all the other kids are playing so competitively, how will kids make the school team if they don't have a lot of practice?

And if kids aren't primed and prepped for kindergarten, if they don't get tutoring in math facts at Kumon, how will they compete with the other kids? Parents who don't shuttle their kids from sports games to Kumon and later to SAT/ACT/math/chemistry/English tutoring will feel like they are slackers. And yet, the race just gets more frenzied with each passing year, as there are more lost moments of youth, more lost papers, more lost chances to find out what kids are really interested in.

In the parts of New York City where I work, kids are often touted as *Olympic material*. If these assessments were accurate, most of the nation's Olympic athletes would have come from the streets of Manhattan, Brooklyn, and New Jersey. This can't be true if history is our guide. When teachers at tony private schools speak about a great sailor or swimmer or skier, they often say "Tokyo 2020, baby," as if the student in question were going to bestow Olympics tickets on his favorite teachers (doubtful). These are kids who tear out of school the minute it ends and head to the pool or who are often absent from school so they can participate in sailing regattas. Their worry tells on their faces. Day in and day out they are in the pool or on the water or on the slopes. There is no doubt they love their sport, but the time involved in perfecting themselves begins to wear them down. There is a time, usually in ninth or tenth grade, when it all becomes too much. They can't handle chemistry and finals and their tournaments at the same time. But their parents keep driving them to early-morning practices and weekend tournaments, and the kids keep doing their homework on planes.

The term *Olympic material* should be banned or at least used with great caution. There are few athletes who get to that level, never mind the pro level. And while sports help some kids get into college, it doesn't help them all. If you want to get your kid into a so-called reach college, there might be better ways to do it. If you can write a check, that might be the best way to stop torturing your child and give to a worthy cause at the university. You will have to think about whether your child would be happier getting into a school on their own merits or having their way paved by Mom and Dad.

There are other ways to gain favored status in admissions that many people forget about. For example, play double-reed instruments like the bassoon and oboe or brass instruments like the baritone horn and French horn or strings like the viola. These instruments are underrepresented among college applicants, and kids won't injure themselves or stay up until late hours playing them, unlike sports. If they are sporty, there are sports that have higher rates of helping people be accepted to college. Girls' ice hockey has the highest rate of enabling high-school athletes to play in college. Boys' hockey and lacrosse are also relatively high, though lower than girls' hockey. Perhaps easiest of all, have your child pick an unusual major like Near Eastern studies or something in the humanities, which are struggling to find students.

The easiest thing a New York City parent can do to get their kid into a better college is to leave New York City, where there are simply too many applicants to prestigious colleges. Or, if one wants to stay in New York, attend a public school where there are fewer applicants to prestigious colleges.

There is one variable that parents tend to overlook when they are hoping to get their children into college. Daniel Eisenberg at the University of Michigan and others have found that mental health predicts success in college. For example, students with depression are more likely to drop out and have lower GPAs, particularly if they also have an anxiety disorder. Mental health affects students' ability to handle school, which in turn affects longer-term outcomes such as employment and income. It's true that exercise in and of itself can be helpful to mental health, but it's not necessary to play on intense travel teams to get the benefit of exercise. Some affluent families are able to get their children adequate mental-health help because they have the means and the willingness to do so. For others, getting mental-health help seems foreign or stigmatizing or takes a back seat to sports.

For many parents, the link between mental health and

life success is not at first easy to grasp, but mental-health problems can prevent even the brightest young adult from reaching their potential. Time spent on the therapist's couch might turn out to be far more critical for young people than time spent studying for the SAT or on the tennis court.

Mental-health problems tend to get worse when kids are in their early twenties, and I've worked with many college students who've had to take time off because their skills and mental health were not in order. Jamie is in his sophomore year at a prestigious liberal-arts college when he begins crushing and smoking Adderall, the stimulant medication he takes for ADHD. His intent is to stay up for many nights in a row to make up the work he had not done for midterms. He spends most of his days on the track team, and he doesn't sleep well, so he needs the extra energy to get through the late-night work. Part of the problem is that, despite having attended a prestigious private high school, he doesn't know how to write an analytical paper. His ideas swirl together in an airy cascade that dissolves into nothing. He talks about ideas, around ideas, and yet nothing winds up on the paper. No one has ever shown him how to get his ideas down, revise them, and organize them—the quotidian parts of writing.

We spend weeks going through each stage of writing a research paper for the class he is taking at NYU. He still needs help crafting each paragraph, and I ask him how he made it through so many years of school without learning to write. "There were always tutors," he says. "And my school allowed me to hand in papers late. It was kind of like 'three strikes and you're still not out'." He feels as though this policy did not help him. "They should have been harder on me," he says in retrospect. I put together the pieces and realize that he must have had tutors write his papers for years—or at least heavily edit them—without teaching him how to write on his own. He returns to college and has tutoring (not from me) to get through his coursework. His therapist, with his parents' permission, tells me that he continues to struggle with depression and with wanting a romantic relationship that he can't seem to manage.

In addition, I've tutored students who have had major depressive and bipolar episodes in college. Some researchers, such as Demitri and Janice Papolos, believe that stress can sensitize the brain to depression or mania. These stressors are called kindling, and like smaller twigs that help logs catch fire, they ignite the brain to be sensitive to mood disruptions that then ignite on their own. Alcohol and some drugs can also be sources of kindling, and a person who has had these types of kindling experiences can then begin to experience them on their own, without the kindling. However, these brain fires can also be doused through treatment, and the teenage and early-adult years represent a time when people can either be set on the path to better mental health or continue to heap their piles of kindling.

The ways in which affluent children are raised today don't give them the time to receive mental-health treatment when needed. I've spoken to many parents who tell me "My child is willing to see a therapist, but the problem is that there is no time." My position, for ethical and practical reasons, is that one needs to make time, though that's easier said than done. The ethical reason is that a child in pain needs help and strategies, and the practical reason is that a child, however bright, cannot function without good mental health. I know myself that it's hard to always find the time to get the treatment one needs, but the early-adult years present a critical juncture in which kids who are faced with troubling mental-health symptoms need to prioritize mental-health help until they have regained a surer footing.

Parents tend to think that college will offer their children the same sorts of support that high school offers, without realizing that the structure of high school is taken away. It's not rare for parents to still wake up their high-school seniors, force them to eat breakfast, and remind them that they have to work on their college applications. This type of external structure disappears in college, and the demands on students to function independently and with greater planning skills increase. It's sometimes hard for parents to see how much help and structure their children are receiving under their roof and to be realistic about whether their son or daughter will actually get out of bed and get to class on their own.

The most critical skills I've seen for college students include the ability to ask professors for help and to make appointment times at the writing center, the ability to get out of bed in the morning, and the ability to do one's laundry. I've been amazed by college-bound students who have received thousands of hours of tutoring and athletic lessons who don't know how to do their laundry, make a simple meal like eggs or pasta, mail a letter, calculate tips, or pay a bill. These skills don't take as much time to teach as other skills do, but they are far more important in many ways.

Perhaps the affluent bank on their kids getting help with these tasks, but they are still necessary for kids to feel capable and functional. I remember one very wealthy mother telling me sheepishly, "My son will learn how to do the laundry in college," but I wasn't sure who would teach him. When possible, I make sure the kids I'm working with have some of these skills down before heading off to college.

I've worked with many students who weren't necessarily fast or agile in the classroom but who have done very well in school and as young professionals by knowing how to get help. Remember Khalil, the boy with the Rolexes? He did very well at a prestigious college precisely because he had extra-time accommodations and had to speak with his professor at the beginning of each semester about his tests and finals. By approaching his professors, he got to know them, and he felt comfortable asking for help. He was one of the lower-ranked students in high school, but he did well in college because he is personable, comfortable with himself, and aware of when he needs to reach out for support. These abilities have stood him in better stead than raw academic talent.

The problem with affluence in children extends far beyond the Upper East Side of Manhattan. Suniya Luthar has studied high-achieving schools across the country. She believes that a child's socioeconomic status does not determine the pressures that face them as much as where they go to school. "Even the kid who lives above the pizza shop" can be subject to these pressures if they attend a high-pressure school, she says.

For years, poverty, discrimination, and trauma have been known risk factors for adolescent mental health. For the first time in 2018, another factor joined the list of major risk factors for kids' emotional well-being: high-achieving schools. The Robert Wood Johnson Foundation added exposure to pressure to succeed as one of the main risk factors for kids. Children raised in high-pressure schools run the risk of psychological disorders and substance abuse, even if they aren't from high-income families. These rates can top those in low-income communities. This means that the kids of the 1 percent are subject to risks even in the context of what looks like benign, supportive environments. A risk factor does not mean that these types of high-pressure environments (which can include public schools like Stuyvesant) cause mental illness or that they aren't fulfilling places for some kids. It does mean that we have to step back and think about the pressures kids in these schools are exposed to and whether all these pressures are healthy and necessary.

How can parents who truly love their kids and value their mental health push them into these types of situations? Luthar believes that parents become coerced into overscheduling their children's lives because the routine of playing in five sports games per week has become the norm in affluent communities. "The community expects you to do this," she says of the parents who overschedule their children, and if the parents don't go to all their kids' games, they "will be the odd person out."

In addition to tackling the poverty, discrimination, and trauma that affect many of our kids, we can also start dialing back the pressures on the young. There are simple things that parents can do. Luthar, who goes into high-achieving schools to conduct surveys, has found that kids who are the most troubled feel that their parents value achievements over personal decency. In other words, kids need to feel that their parents support them, even if they don't achieve. "The parents need to be a buffer providing a sense of balance," Luthar says, "and they need to stop thinking of the hockey game like it's the Olympics." Teachers, coaches, and administrators can also play a role in emphasizing decency and integrity over achievement.

The athletic industrial complex that recruits the young has burgeoned into a $15 billion industry. This sector, which has grown 55 percent since 2010, has prospered like a weed, and major players in professional sports are involved in investing in youth sports. It's all good news for investors but not such good news for kids, who get home at eleven thirty at night after grueling practices, or for parents, who spend tens of thousands of dollars a year on travel teams. Some kids aren't even good enough to make varsity teams at their schools, but their parents pay money to send them to tournaments that cause them to miss school. At the same time, low-key, free or lower-cost sports opportunities such as Little League are declining.

We need to start a nuclear freeze on these kinds of sports for our kids. It has become an arms race in which any form of reason has gone out the window, replaced by a new norm of frenzy and delusion. Many parents spend so much trying to get their kids college scholarships that they would have been better off putting this money in the bank. Some parents even have apps that help them manage weekend games for multiple kids. Doesn't any parent miss family time or at least a break for salsa and chips in the afternoon ? This generation of kids is paying the price for this lack of balance.

Parents wonder if their children will just vegetate and play video games in the absence of organized sports, and this is perhaps a real concern. But increasingly, communities are bringing back local leagues that enable kids to play sports but on a more rational schedule that allows them time with their friends, time with their family and community, and time to do schoolwork.

Is it too idealistic to hope that we can relax the pressure in well-off communities? Luthar has been involved in consulting with the affluent community of Wilton, Connecticut, through her nonprofit Authentic Connections. The results of a survey in Wilton found that about 30 percent of the kids in the high school had internalizing symptoms, such as anxiety, sadness, depression, and somatic complaints such as stomachaches. The national rate is about 7 percent. Wilton decided to do something about it. Students led initiatives to tell others about mental health, and even younger kids were trained in how to build resilience. Some of the parents decided to change their kids' schedules to make them less cluttered, and they found less fighting with parents was the happy result.

The American dream as it now stands—the one Gatsby himself wanted so badly as he stared at the green light on Daisy Buchanan's pier—has gaping holes in it. Money can make life glittering, magical, fresh, until it creates loneliness and lovelessness in the young.

Perhaps the new American dream can involve an element of contentment. We are a restless nation, one whose success has been predicated on an itch to get going, to be constantly moving. There is something charming about our capacity for change, but I can't help wondering what it would have been like if Gatsby had been content in his dazzling West Egg mansion. Instead of always looking across the water to Daisy's pier, he had found happiness at home. It was not in his nature. Is it in ours, or can we make it so for our children?

10

Farewell, My Lovely

"The food is so good in Crete," Sophie's grandmother tells me for the fifth time. "Sophie will show you when you visit!" I'm sitting next to her at Sophie's graduation, trying to keep my eye on Sophie as she is called up to get her diploma in the chapel next to her school, but Yaya, as her granddaughter calls her, can't stop speaking about Greece. While we are waiting for the graduates to walk in, she tells me about growing up there after World War II, when the country was devastated. "My husband and I went upstate, and we opened a restaurant. Sophie's mother grew up serving!"

Sophie's Yaya is a diminutive woman, neatly dressed in a navy blue suit and silk shirt. She wears an evil-eye necklace encrusted with diamonds and sapphires, and her husband, even smaller, wears a short-sleeved white shirt tucked into his pants with a belt. He reads the program for the graduation again and again, nudging his wife to show her Sophie's name and the asterisk that indicates that she is part of the honor society.

"My husband and I didn't go to college," she tells me. "Sophie's mom got a scholarship. We paid for part of it, but now, Sophie is going to the Ivy League!" I don't want to correct her to explain that Sophie's school is a Seven Sister, once the equivalent of the Ivy League for women, as she seems so attached to the idea of the Ivy League. It is for this she has been serving lumberjack breakfasts for the past quarter of a century.

After the graduation ceremony, Sophie invites me to her parents' apartment. Her mother has catered the event, but the grandparents insist on making Greek specialties and serving them to me and Sophie's friends. "This is spanakopita," the grandmother explains. "You have to eat this when you visit me." Sophie's grandmother has graciously extended me an invitation to stop by her kitchen at any time.

Until attending graduation, I had never met Sophie's grandparents, who live in upstate New York, and I had no idea that they still run a diner or that they speak Greek as their first language. Sophie's mom does not speak Greek to her daughter, but Sophie is planning to visit her relatives in Greece over the summer and hopes to pick some up. Sophie's mother pitches herself into socializing and appearing in society photographs in magazines and on websites. Now I know that she learned to socialize at a Greek diner upstate—not at Miss Porter's as I had assumed. Her status is the result of hard work, not inheritance, and she wants to protect it for her daughter.

Trevor's father and I have one final conversation before Trevor leaves for college. I ask him how he thinks his son will do at the Ivy he is heading to, and the father says simply, "If I could get through it, he can." That's the only indication I have that Trevor's father might also have struggled in school, maybe also with ADHD or learning issues. It gives a new cast to his unwillingness to allow his son to have extra-time accommodations on tests and the unbending steeliness with which he has raised him. I evaluate him in a softer way, as he makes some muffled remark about how "my all-boys' high school certainly didn't prepare me for college." His implication is that he got through it somehow, probably white-knuckling it all the time, and that his son can too and will be a better person for having done so.

I have worked with parents long enough to know when they are intolerant of their children's lapses not because their children are different from them but because they are the same. In supervising Trevor's spotty academic career, his father has relived his own past. It is now crystal clear to me. I see the way he yelled at Trevor after his lost soccer games in a totally different light—one that is far more illuminating of the father–son dynamic but also far more complex. Still, I have major reservations about Trevor being sent to a school where he will feel lesser than others. It's not clear whether he knows that his father paid for his admission, and I certainly won't be the one to tell him.

Trevor's family doesn't really communicate with me after that point, and when I email them to ask how he is doing, they respond in breezy terms that he's "just great." I can never put together the whole picture of how he's doing; it is kept hazy and removed from me, but I gather from pictures he posts on Facebook that he is in a fraternity and parties a lot. He graduates on time, and I suspect that he has used some kinds of tutors to get through some of his economics and writing-heavy classes.

I see Trevor again during college, at the funeral of his cousin Julia, who had spent time with him on their family's island, where they were close. She went to college full of life and fun. She had struggled with drugs in high school, and her parents had sent her to a rehab program in California for the summer—a program so lavish that teachers at her school, in a fit of dark humor, all said they too wished for a drug problem. The program seemed to work. What's not clear is whether her death was accidental or intentional. She had surely struggled with impulsivity, with depression, with feeling as though she couldn't please her parents, based on my observations and those of her teachers. But she also seemed to be a lover of life, a soccer player, a young woman known for generosity and infectious humor. She held secrets, maybe, that no one knew about, and she chose never to date but only to have one-night flings. She often acted without thinking, it's true. When she was a sophomore in high school, she was suspended for getting into a yelling match with her Spanish teacher. She was contrite afterward, and she and the teacher became close. She had also gotten in trouble for working with a tutor who wrote her papers for her—before she worked with me.

When I attend the funeral on the Upper East Side, the crowd is so large that it's impossible to get into the sanctuary. Instead, I stand outside. Each time one of Julia's former teachers shows up, tears come to my eyes because of the unwritten message telegraphed between us: *I can't believe we're meeting here.* Her friends come pouring out of the church, and I hug the ones I know without speaking. There is literally nothing we can say to each other. Trevor is serious and wears sunglasses but says nothing. He now works as an analyst at a major Wall Street bank, working long hours. He is still dating the woman who reminds me of the Duchess of Cambridge. He never went west.

After the funeral, Julia's former teachers, who have attended the service, huddle outside the church after the family has gone to the grave site. "Was she depressed?" one of them asks me. "You would know."

"I don't know," I say. I was perhaps fooled by Julia's dancing green eyes and her deep laugh. Her anger and impetuousness betrayed her, and she was too willing to argue and to show impatience with her teachers, parents, and friends. Anger can be a sign of deeper depression.

"It must have been hard to be her," the teacher says, "with that father." Julia's father is the Earl of Grantham's brother, and they are both stewards of the family's wealth. But that doesn't solve the mystery. One thing I've learned from working with the children of Fifth Avenue is that the way they appear and the way they really are can be totally different. Julia will forever guard her mysteries, and I will continue to think of her often without coming to any resolution. I vacillate between ruling her death an accident—the

result of a night's partying with prescription painkillers—
and believing that she was tormented and acted lighthearted
as a cover-up. There is also the possibility that both things
are true or that neither is true. I make endless mental loops
and come up with nothing.

I still wonder about Trevor, as he grows up to assume
the family mantle. He has a buoyant attitude, but he has
slipped into his father's shoes. He lives downtown, placing
some distance between him and his father, who lives on
the Upper East Side, but his life seems, so far, to be moving along the same track.

Occasionally, Trevor gets to visit his maternal grandfather out west. His grandfather developed a city in Okla-
homa after starting with tract housing. His grandfather is
unlike the Earl of Grantham—he's a free spirit who is cur-
rently giving away a lot of his earnings. I hope that one day,
Trevor can get out west and work with him, the man who
gave him the marlin that used to hang in his room.

College is generally a breeze for the kids I've worked
with. Burned-out, they choose easy majors—those for
which they've already done the work in high school. One
of my students majors in American history precisely because he already did about 85 percent of the reading in his
high-pressured AP history class during junior year of high
school. It makes me wonder why the classes in high school
had to be so demanding to the point at which the students
completed most of college before they had even set foot on
campus.

When I went to Harvard for college, I was gobsmacked.
I loved being on the campus. I loved taking classes that

had complicated, ironic names like The Myth of America instead of English 11, as classes were called in my public high school. For the first year, I literally had no idea of what people were speaking about, as I wasn't familiar with most prep schools (where many of the students came from) and thought squash was a tasteless vegetable rather than a sport. I had never met so many New Yorkers before. I envied their insouciance and their ability to eat out so much in Harvard Square. (I was on a budget.) I had no idea what Indian food was. Attending a pro forma meeting about plagiarism with all the other first-year students, I thought God was going to smite me down if I unwittingly forgot to paraphrase. I went to most hockey games because I didn't know what else to do.

Strangely, miraculously, I did very well. Not because I was necessarily so smart but because I was hungry. I spent hours upon hours trying to sort out the colonial histories of different African nations for a history class. I went to my teaching assistant's office hours, though I was frightened of her, after I had received a C on my first writing assignment. Everything was exciting. I loved the glow of the streetlights on Harvard Yard where the first-year students lived and believed it had a kind of Baker-Street ambience. I found my own carrel deep in the bowels of the library, where I read *Ulysses*, or at least some of it, and marveled at every word in *Mrs. Dalloway*. I spent an entire weekend reading Ford Madox Ford with a friend of mine, only stopping to eat. I'd never had a friend who savored forty-eight hours of reading as much as I did. I met students who had met Gorbachev, meaning I was one degree of separation away from the architect of perestroika.

In short, it was all new to me, and I had reserves of energy that had not been tapped and the sense that the best of life lay ahead. I could not believe my good luck in moving from rural Massachusetts to Cambridge. It is different for the private school kids from NYC. By the time they arrive on their college campus, they've read many of the books, taken far harder exams, met famous people, partied hard, and seen a great deal of the world. For them, such worldliness easily becomes world-weariness. But peak moments should come rarely so they are savored. Their minds have already been drained, and the first year of college is high-school redux. They procrastinate, they take classes that they don't find that interesting, and they force themselves into majors like economics because they are told to go into banking. Often, they don't show up to class, and occasionally, they flunk finals. They don't fail because they are not prepared. It's because they are overly prepared. They've overtrained, which any marathon runner will tell you is a colossal mistake. Runners have to pace themselves, and so do kids.

Long after I stop working with them, my former students and their families have a way of popping up in unexpected places. Before I leave New York, I see them on the street, particularly when I am downtown near Wall Street. Many work in banks, just like their parents. When I look up their profiles on LinkedIn, I find that most of my male students—and many of my female students—were economics majors in college and now are working as analysts in banks or companies that marry tech and finance: *fintech*. If they have advanced degrees, they are MBAs. A few are in corporate law. Very few have strayed from the traditional path.

When I get the chance to speak with my former students, they remember little of the past. They are comfortably settled on the future and their new points of reference. Though some don't look that different, they walk differently, having thrown off most of their discomfort. They don't yet have the older person's desire to reminisce or the distance from what they went through. Having returned to the city the minute college is over, they have put no distance between themselves and New York. This is where they feel most at home.

"I was terrified of squirrels," one student tells me of his time in Vermont. He walks at night in Midtown, where the crime rate is among the highest in the city.

They start to assume the lives of their parents, or what their parents were thirty years before. The chic area has shifted to downtown and Brooklyn, and I see them on the streets of Dumbo and heading to Crown Heights. They settle in gentrified neighborhoods that are rapidly coming to resemble the Upper East Side, the Upper West Side, and the neighborhoods of their youth. They are places where you can get strong, expensive matcha before heading to yoga classes. The twentysomethings reconnect with others they knew in school, and their lives intersect and reintersect with their former school friends as they interview for jobs, attend graduate school, and send their kids to private school.

Unlike the majority who go into business or law, Sophie dreams of being an actress. A cipher at times, she seems to have the skills for it, and she has a prodigious memory to recall lines, just as she used to cram information about Kievan Rus into her brain. One of her friends has made it big, becoming a model and actress, and I see her face staring out at me from billboards along the New Jersey Turnpike, her beautiful eyes, though without spectacles, shining like Dr. T. J. Eckleburg in *The Great Gatsby*.

Lily becomes confident, a black-clad lover of the arts, and she works as an intern at the Metropolitan Museum. She and Lisa are photographed at society events in galleries and museums. Lily has never stopped craving a new dress, but now, her clothes have acquired an air of sophistication. She wears thick black glasses and styles her hair in a messy ponytail. Once nicely plump, she has become anemically thin like her mother. She lives at home for now, which she says is simply because her parents' apartment is near the Museum Mile. She plans to work as a museum curator or in an art gallery. She sews all the time, remaking her clothes into what she wants them to be. She can take a garment and rip it apart at the seams. She has been able to craft her clothes, and her reality, into something that is at least beginning to match up to her internal vision.

Other students I taught or tutored or just knew show up in the society pages of the tabloids. One is dating a famous actor, and then the relationship is off. Ben, once touted as one of Fifth Avenue's most eligible bachelors, falls off the social radar, though his mother still religiously attends society events. Ben does not seem to have any kind of job, as far as I can tell, and I wonder if his family inheritance came through after all. Some of the parents I used to work with show up as guests at Meghan Markle's wedding to Prince Harry. I see them on TV and think they look older under their fascinators. Part of me wishes that my students had become freer spirits, and in my less charitable moments, I wish that the students who became beautiful writers weren't all on Wall Street. I dream of going to a former student's book-launch party, but it hasn't happened yet.

While I know my students and their stories will always be a part of me, after nearly fifteen years of tutoring and teaching in the city, I feel it is time to leave New York with my husband and now-teenage son. While I am tenacious and used to waging long wars for what I want, this city has defeated me. It has woken me up in the middle of the night, not from an alarm or blaring music—which I've long ago learned to tune out—but from anxiety. My adrenal glands are shot. It has also warped my perceptions so that I feel, next to the people I tutor (save the students I tutor pro bono), poor. I know that I am nothing but privileged and that my entire sense of the cosmos is out of whack. My son's sensory systems are overwhelmed in the city, particularly when we live in the valley of ashes along the LaGuardia flight path, and a move to somewhere quieter will do us all good. While packing, I carefully store every thank-you note a student has ever written me in a small box, which I keep in the sock drawer of my dresser. I take the letters out to read them again sometimes.

Leaving the city for Massachusetts, I drive by a girl at a bus stop with her dog-eared copy of *The Great Gatsby* open while wearing Beats headphones. I wonder where she is in the book, if she has yet driven through the valley of ashes or seen Gatsby's collapsing pile of linen shirts on his bed.

I am not like Nick in the end. He understood Gatsby. I have merely learned alongside Gatsby's children. They are still teaching me all that I have yet to fully understand.

★ ★ ★ ★ ★

ENDNOTES

Chapter 1:

Information on vaping:
www.nih.gov/news-events/news-releases/teens-using-vaping-devices-record-numbers.

Chapter 2:

Saez and Zucman research:
https://review.chicagobooth.edu/economics/2017/article/never-mind-1-percent-lets-talk-about-001-percent.

Where the 1 percent lives:
www.citylab.com/life/2011/10/where-one-percent-live/393/ and www.cnbc.com/2018/08/08/where-the-highest-earners-in-america-live.html.

Most affluent people having the largest families:
https://qz.com/1125805/the-reason-the-richest-women-in-the-us-are-the-ones-having-the-most-kids.

Who goes to private school:
www.gse.harvard.edu/news/18/10/harvard-edcast-who-goes-private-school.

Murnane, Richard, Sean Reardon, Preeya Mbekeani, and Anne Lamb. "Who Goes to Private Schools." Education Next 18:4 (Autumn 2018): 59–66.

After-school activities of affluent children:
Gilbert S. "For Some Children, It's an After-school Pressure Cooker." New York Times. August 3, 1999 :F7.

Social mobility of children:
https://fivethirtyeight.com/features/rich-kids-stay-rich-poor-kids-stay-poor.

Chapter 3:

Praising kids and Carol Dweck:
www.theatlantic.com/education/archive/2016/12/how-praise-became-a-consolation-prize/510845.

Overindulgence of children:
Bredehoft, D. J., S. A. Mennicke, A. M. Potter, and J. I. Clarke, 1998. "Perceptions Attributed by Adults to Parental Overindulgence during Childhood." Journal of Family and Consumer Sciences Education, 16(2), 3-17.

Chapter 4:

Quotes from Suniya Luthar:
Interview with Suniya Luthar, 9/14/2019.

Substance use among affluent children:
Suniya S. Luthar, Phillip J. Small, Lucia Ciciolla. Adolescents from upper middle class communities: Substance misuse and addiction across early adulthood. Development and Psychopathology, 2017; 1 DOI: 10.1017/S0954579417000645.

Chapter 5:

Clinton Trowbridge at Groton:
Trowbridge, Clinton. Grotties Don't Kiss. Vineyard Press, 2002.

Chapter 6:

Disordered eating among athletes:
Williams, Gemma, 2016. "Binge Eating and Binge Eating Disorder in Athletes: A Review of Theory and Evidence." http://thesportjournal.org/article/binge-eating-and-binge-eating-disorder-in-athletes-a-review-of-theory-and-evidence.

Research by Paul Piff and colleagues:
Piff, Paul K., Daniel M. Stancato, Stéphane Côté, Rodolfo Mendoza-Denton, and Dacher Keltner. "Higher Social Class Predicts Increased Unethical Behavior." Proceedings of the National Academy of Sciences, March 2012, 109(11), 4086–4091; DOI:10.1073/pnas.1118373109.

www.businessinsider.com/rich-people-more-likely-to-steal-cheat-lie-2018-8.

Piff, Paul K., M. W. Kraus, S. Côté, B. H. Cheng, and D. Keltner, 2010. "Having Less, Giving More: The Influence of Social Class on Prosocial Behavior." Journal of Personality and Social Psychology, 99(5), 771–784.

Chapter 8:

SAT predictive value:
Culpepper, Steven, and Charles Pierce, 2016. "Differential Prediction Generalization in College Admissions Testing." Journal of Educational Psychology. *https://doi.org/10.1037/edu0000104.*

Chapter 9:

Mental health in college:
Eisenberg, Daniel, Ezra Golberstein, and Justin Hunt, 2009. "Mental Health and Academic Success in College." The B.E. Journal of Economic Analysis & Policy. 9 (1): Article 40.

Research on bipolar disorder:
Papolos, D., and J. Papolos, 1999. The Bipolar Child. New York, NY: Broadway Books.

Suniya Luthar and Robert Wood Johnson Foundation:
https://psychcentral.com/news/2018/10/29/parent-child-bond-tied-to-mental-health-of-teens-in-high-achieving-schools/139911.html.

Interview with Suniya Luthar, 9/14/2019.

Stats about travel teams:
Gregory, Sean. "How Sports Became a $15 Billion Industry."
Time, August 24, 2017.

Information about program in Wilton, CT:
www.npr.org/sections/health-shots/2018/06/11/616900580/
back-off-how-to-get-out-of-the-high-pressure-parenting-
trap.

Research on affluent children:
Kindlon, D., 2001. Too Much of a Good Thing: Raising
Children in an Indulgent Age. New York, N.Y.: Hyperion.

Levine, M., 2006. The Price of Privilege: How Parental Pres-
sure and Material Advantage Are Creating a Generation of
Disconnected and Unhappy Kids. New York, N.Y.: Harper-
Collins.

Twenge, J. M., 2006. Generation Me: Why Today's Young
Americans Are More Confident, Assertive, Entitled and More
Miserable Than Ever Before. New York, N.Y.: Free Press.

ACKNOWLEDGMENTS

This book—and I—would be nothing without the hundreds of students, teachers, and parents I've worked with over the years. The process of learning and teaching is a circular, unpredictable, and occasionally enlightening one, and it's brought me moments of profound gratitude. There are those rare times when I know that I've broken through to a kid, and many, many more in which I just relish the humor-filled journey. I recall one of the best teachers I know saying to her class, "That's why we love you students so much—we get to be around all your young energy." People who teach are recipients of a kind of uplifting, unjaded spirit. We're far more fortunate at times than the students, who don't, after all, have a choice about their presence in the classroom. I hope all my students, past, present, and future, know how grateful I am for the chance to learn from new generations, TikTok and all. I do keep your notes in my sock drawer. And to the teachers I've worked with over the years, I relish your excitement about learning and your warm companionship while we try to see kids through the troubles of teenagerdom.

Thanks to the brilliant and patient Jessica Papin, my agent at Dystel, Goderich & Bourret, who shepherded the proposal through so many drafts, and to my equally brilliant editorial team, Peter Joseph and Grace Towery at Hanover Square Press. I knew that I would thoroughly enjoy working with Peter the first moment we spoke, and his logical mind and knowledge of literary allusions are awe-inspiring. Grace is an amazingly talented wordsmith and editor, and her words of encouragement meant a great deal. The amazing copyeditor, Vanessa Wells, caught my every mistaken reference and usage.

I've spent a long time thinking about my childhood while writing this book, and I feel really lucky to have grown up with the Grossbergs—Mom, Dad, and brother Josh. The moments we spent doing really stupid things like the circle dance, "Aingeing," and trying to understand Estonian are what grounded me in life. I'm glad I grew up in the '70s and acquired a kind of dark New England humor. My family now, Teddy and John, are equally strange and lovable. I'd have nothing to write about or celebrate without you.